DATE DUE

SURVIVING
AN AFFAIR

Other books by Willard F. Harley, Jr.

His Needs, Her Needs
Love Busters
5 Steps to Romantic Love
Give and Take
Your Love and Marriage
The Four Gifts of Love

SURVIVING
AN AFFAIR

DR. WILLARD F. HARLEY, JR.

AND

DR. JENNIFER HARLEY CHALMERS

Fleming H. Revell
A Division of Baker Book House
Grand Rapids, Michigan 49516

Published by Fleming H. Revell
a division of Baker Book House Company
P.O. Box 6287, Grand Rapids, MI 49516-6287

Printed in the United States of America

Library of Congress Cataloging-in-Publication Data

Harley, Willard F.
    Surviving an affair / Willard F. Harley, Jr., Jennifer Harley Chalmers.
        p. cm.
    ISBN 0-8007-1758-9 (cloth)
    1. Adultery. 2. Marriage. 3. Marriage counseling. I. Chalmers, Jennifer Harley. II. Title
    HQ806.H36 1998
    306.73'6—dc21   98-24531

For current information about all releases from Baker Book House, visit our web site:
http://www.bakerbooks.com

To
Joyce and Phil

CONTENTS

You Can Survive This Affair

I f you are a victim of infidelity, you have been on the emotional roller coaster ride of your life. Most couples caught up in the tragedy of an affair tell us that they have never felt such intense emotions. They are overwhelmed by anger, depression, fear, guilt, loneliness, and shame.

A betrayed spouse will ask, *How could my spouse do this to me— cheating on me, lying to me over and over again? I can never trust my spouse again. I have so much anger and resentment it scares me. My feelings go way beyond hurt—I can't even put into words the pain I am feeling.*

A wayward spouse often says, *I used to beg my spouse for more attention but I never beg anymore—my lover gives me all the attention I need. But I don't know if the attention I'm getting is worth the price. One moment I'm sure I've done the right thing. Then I look into the faces of my children and I'm not sure anymore. I don't want to give up my family but if I give up my lover, I'll be losing the best thing that ever happened to me. What should I do? I'm an emotional wreck!*

When a couple feel such strong emotions, many question if marital reconciliation is possible. *How can we ever recover from such pain? And even if we recover, can we live with the memory of betrayal? Can we ever trust each other again? Can we ever love each other again?*

As marriage counselors we have been asked these questions thousands of times and have been able to respond with a definite *yes*. Let us assure you that if you put into practice what we recommend in this book, the prognosis for the future of your marriage is very good.

In the pages that follow, we use "I" to refer to either of us as we describe our experiences and counsel.

It's Hard to Believe That Marital Recovery Is Possible after an Affair

When I first counseled spouses that were trapped in an affair, I thought I would be preparing them for divorce. But to my surprise, again and again I saw opportunities to save marriages. Infidelity did not necessarily cause either the betrayed spouse or the wayward spouse to want a divorce. Often what they both wanted was to escape the pain of their mistake and create a thriving marriage.

> The path that leads to recovery is very narrow, and unless couples find that path, the tragedy of an affair can permanently cripple a marriage and often leads to the further tragedy of divorce.

So that became my mission—to help couples recover from the disaster of an affair and create a fulfilling marriage that would prevent any future affairs. Since I began helping these tormented couples, I've witnessed the recovery of thousands of marriages. But the path that leads to recovery is very narrow, and unless couples find that path, the tragedy of an affair can permanently cripple a marriage and often leads to the further tragedy of divorce.

If you are a wayward spouse or a betrayed spouse, you may be undecided as to what to do next. One moment you want to divorce your spouse, and the next you want to try to reconcile. That's the way most people in your situation feel because there are advantages and disadvantages to both choices. Divorce carries with it the destruction of a family and the loss of a spouse you may still love, and yet reconciliation means you will be living with the scars of betrayal and the risk of another affair. Your emotional reactions may be so strong that you simply cannot make the choice right now.

Even if you have decided that marital reconciliation is impossible, or if it's only you or only your spouse who wants to survive the affair and restore your marriage, I would like you to consider my strategy for recovery. It has proven successful for thousands of couples, and once you understand its objectives, you may be willing to try it. My plan is that narrow path that gets you beyond the affair, helps you make your marriage better than it's ever been, and protects you from future affairs.

You Can Do Better than Survive—Your Marriage Can Thrive

There is hope for the recovery of your marriage, and thousands of couples have proven it. When you complete my program for reconciliation, you will have the marriage you have always wanted— one that is filled with love and compatibility.

> My plan is that narrow path that gets you beyond the affair, helps you make your marriage better than it's ever been, and protects you from future affairs.

Before I tell you about my plan for recovery, you need to know some of the common characteristics of affairs. I want to tell you about Jon and Sue. Their situation may be different from yours but it illustrates some of the basic elements of most affairs. Like so many couples, Jon and Sue thought it could never happen to them.

It Could Never Happen to Me!

Jon and Sue were about to celebrate their eighth anniversary and had good reason to celebrate. They had two healthy daughters and a beautiful home and Jon had just been promoted to a new position that increased his salary by almost 50 percent. That extra income allowed Sue to cut back on her hours at work so that she could spend more time with their children.

Sue was content with her life. She enjoyed the comfortable home and other luxuries that Jon's income was able to provide. She worked as a part-time special education teacher, allowing her time to do what she loved most—raising her children. But when it came to her relationship with Jon, the romance was gone. Sometimes she day-dreamed about the times they had spent talking to each other, showing their affection for each other, and making love with passion and excitement. But with his new job, there was no time for that. Besides, Sue's life was enjoyable in so many other ways that she thought she could overlook the loss of Jon's companionship.

Jon was also content. He loved his wife and children and was proud of the quality of life he was able to provide them. His new job was enjoyable and challenging, although it required most of his time. He wanted to spend more time with Sue and his children but he and Sue had both agreed that their time to be together would come after he was more established in his career.

Jon was an achiever, and Sue loved that trait in a man. In fact she had married him partly because she knew he was ambitious and would provide well for her and their children. She had encouraged him to accept the responsibilities that led to his advancement. Sue wanted Jon to reach his highest potential but she didn't understand that the time he spent away from her prevented him from reaching his potential as her husband.

On the evening of their anniversary celebration, Sue and Jon exchanged cards and gifts that expressed their love for each other. Then they went to dinner at their favorite restaurant, where Jon had asked Sue to marry him.

But something wasn't right. Sue felt uncomfortable talking to Jon. Their conversation about their children, his work, her work, and even about their plans for the future all seemed contrived and forced. She felt so distant from Jon that it was as if she hardly knew him.

When they returned home, Jon expected to end the evening making love to Sue, but to his astonishment, she was not interested. Jon and Sue had agreed from the beginning of their marriage that sex was never to be a ritual. It was to be an expression of their true feelings, something they did when they both felt a sexual passion for each other. But though Sue and Jon had been out together on their anniversary, Sue still felt lonely and certainly not passionate. When she told Jon she wasn't interested in sex, he went to sleep very disappointed.

The next day Sue felt guilty about the way their anniversary had ended and called her husband three times to tell him how bad she felt. She blamed it all on having been in a bad mood that week and tried to assure Jon that it wasn't anything he had done to upset her. But she was at a loss to know what was causing the problem or what to do about it. The passion was simply gone.

So instead of admitting her lack of feeling for Jon, Sue made love to him the next night, even though she did it because of guilt, not passion. What's worse, she pretended to enjoy the experience as much as she had in the past. She decided that it was unrealistic to have sex with Jon only when she felt passionate.

Sue didn't tell Jon how she now felt about sex. So he assumed that whatever was bothering her on their anniversary had ended and everything was back to normal again. In fact after their anniversary Sue saw to it that they made love more often than before, which made Jon very happy.

Sue, though, began to feel restless and bored with her life. When a friend suggested that she volunteer for the Lake Restoration Committee, she jumped at the opportunity. Sue and Jon were both concerned about the way development was affecting the quality of the lake that bordered their community. The committee met monthly and Sue enjoyed being part of a group that was doing such important work. She became friends with several of the committee members and developed a particularly good friendship with Greg.

It was so easy for Sue to talk with Greg at the meetings. They usually sat together and he was always very friendly and cheerful. He listened attentively to her ideas, rarely interrupted her, and discussed issues with her in a respectful and supportive way. In fact, he usually came to her defense when others disagreed with her opinions.

Between meetings Greg often called Sue at home to discuss committee business, and once in a while they would meet for lunch. The more she got to know Greg, the more she looked forward to his calls and their lunch dates.

Greg had been divorced for three years and had custody of his two boys who were five and seven, close to the ages of Sue's children. Sue admired him for the good job he did caring for his children without the help of a wife. But she also felt sorry for him bearing all of the burden himself, so she offered to help him care for his boys if he was ever stuck.

At first, Sue told Jon about her friendship with Greg. When she had lunch with Greg or watched his children in an emergency, Jon knew about it. Jon had lunch with women from work once in a while, so he could not see a problem with Sue having lunch with a man. Besides, he trusted Sue. He believed that she would never be unfaithful to him. And Sue would never have imagined that she could be unfaithful to Jon.

But as Sue's friendship with Greg deepened, she became increasingly secretive about it. She knew that if she were completely honest about how much time she was spending with Greg, Jon would become alarmed and encourage her to put a stop to it. She told herself she had a right to a friendship with a man, and that she could handle it. Besides, Jon didn't usually ask her what she did during the day, so she seldom had to lie. She simply didn't talk about her growing secret life.

Within a few months of Sue and Jon's anniversary dinner, Greg had become more than just a friend to Sue. She had fallen in love with him, and Greg was in love with her. Sue could not remember ever feeling so attracted to a man, not even to Jon. Greg made her feel beautiful, interesting, desirable, and alive.

The secret life, however, could not remain a secret forever. It came crashing into the open when Jon decided to surprise Sue by returning home two days early from one of his many business trips. It was late, and the children were asleep. He quietly entered the house and went to his bedroom with flowers and candy in his arms. There he found Sue—and Greg! Greg grabbed his clothes and ran out of the house, leaving Sue alone to try to explain what had happened.

The Dangerous Illusion: It Could Never Happen to Me

In their eight years of marriage, neither Jon nor Sue ever thought they would be the victims of infidelity until it actually happened. They had friends who had been unfaithful to a spouse, but Sue and Jon felt they could never betray each other's trust that way and they believed their moral standards set them apart from those who yield to the temptation of an affair.

Spouses who have not experienced an affair firsthand are usually very trusting. They don't believe that infidelity could ever infect their marriage. I often hear, "My spouse could never be unfaithful—she has my utmost trust," and "He has such strong moral convictions that an affair is unthinkable."

When a spouse has an affair, it usually comes as a complete surprise even to him or her. That person often reports, "I had always regarded those who had affairs as selfish, misguided fools with no discipline whatsoever. I could not have imagined having an affair myself."

But infidelity is something that doesn't just happen on afternoon soaps. It happens in most marriages. *MOST* marriages, you may ask? Yes, unfortunately, most marriages.

> Infidelity is something that doesn't just happen on afternoon soaps. It happens in most marriages.

As common as an affair is in marriage, it is always devastating to almost everyone involved. It's one of the most painful experiences that the betrayed spouse will ever be forced to endure, and it is trau-matic for the children. Friends and members of the extended fam-ily usually suffer as well. But what most people don't realize is that the wayward spouse and the lover are also hurt by the experience. They almost always suffer from acute depression, often with thoughts of suicide. With all of the sadness and suffering, why do so many people have an affair?

The answer is that, for the moment, it seems to be the right thing to do. Men and women are easily carried away by their emotions, making the worst mistakes of their lives.

One would think that at least the people with strong religious con-victions and moral commitments would have special protection from extramarital affairs. Yet I have counseled hundreds of people with these convictions who were not able to resist unfaithfulness. Just observing the many religious leaders who have succumbed to the temptation of infidelity proves to me that under certain condi-tions infidelity is irresistible.

The truth is that infidelity doesn't necessarily develop out of a bankrupt system of moral values. Instead, personal values change to accommodate the affair. What had been inconceivable prior to an affair can actually seem reasonable and even morally right after an affair. Many people who have always believed in being faithful in marriage find that their values do not protect them when they are faced with the temptation of an affair.

It became clear to me early in my counseling experience that affairs were much more common than I had ever imagined. But now, after years of marriage counseling, I have come to realize that almost everyone, given the right conditions, would have an affair.

Sue's Side of the Story

I never thought I would be unfaithful to Jon. I had always looked at people who had affairs as moral weaklings. But my view has changed. Now I understand how important it is to be with the one you love, even if your friends and family don't approve. And I have a new appreciation for others who have affairs.

I broke my vow of fidelity and feel very guilty about it. Jon wants to work things out and get our marriage back on track, but I would rather die than leave Greg. I now believe my marriage to Jon was a mistake because I did not understand what love really is. I never would have married Jon if I had known Greg first. We will be soul mates for the rest of our lives.

I feel guilty and ashamed of what I have done, and even what I am thinking, but nevertheless my feelings for Greg are powerful and undeniable. I have tried to forget about him but I can't do it. Greg rekindled feelings in me that have been dormant for a long time. I find myself thinking about him often and wish I could always be with him.

Jon is a good man and doesn't deserve what I've done to him. I know he loves me. But I cannot remain married to a man I don't love, even though a divorce would probably be hard on our children. If I were to lose Greg, I would lose my soul and my spirit. He has become a part of me, a part I cannot abandon or ignore. Even if I never see Greg again, he will be in my heart for the rest of my life.

Most unfaithful spouses see an affair as enlightenment. They did not know what they were missing until the affair revealed it to them. In many cases a spouse is feeling depressed and unfulfilled, and the affair changes that. What had been missing in his or her life is found, and it's a wonderful relief. What years of therapy can't achieve is instantly accomplished whenever the lover is present—happiness and fulfillment.

But in some cases, prior to an affair, a spouse is not depressed. Sue, for example, was content with her life. The only sign of her vulnerability was that she no longer felt like making love to her husband. Her passion was gone, leaving a void that Greg willingly filled.

Sue did not develop a friendship with Greg because she wanted him as her lover. She simply needed a friend. And she never intended for their friendship to develop into an affair. She trusted herself to be faithful to Jon. But Greg did such a good job caring for her, that he met her important emotional needs, and she fell in love with him.

What made Sue's relationship with Greg seem so right was that it was unplanned. It just "happened." That's why Sue felt that Greg was meant to be her lover, because she had not done anything to encourage it. They simply found each other and when they did, they each thought they had found their soul mate.

Jon's Side of the Story

Jon, of course, was blown away by what he saw when he returned from his trip. He had no idea that Sue was having an affair. It seemed like a very bad dream from which he would eventually wake up. But after a few days passed, he had to face the truth. He knew that he had been betrayed by the one he trusted most in life, his wife. She had hurt him more than he could have ever imagined. This is how Jon described his feelings to me:

When we first married, Sue and I made an agreement with each other that we would always be honest about our feelings. I trusted her and never doubted her word. Now I will never believe a thing she says to me again.

Ever since I've known her, she has cared about the way people feel. She can't even hurt a bug. Yet she has chosen to hurt me, the one she promised to care for the most. I thought I knew her but I guess I never did. How could I have not seen through her deceit? How could I have been so blind?

Sue and I both worked very hard to build a good life for ourselves and our children. I admit that I have not been with her much these past few years. I could have done a better job helping her raise our children too. But we talked about all of that and she agreed with me that what I was doing was best for all of us. I didn't complain to her about the sacrifices I was making for our future, and she didn't complain to me, either. We just did what we felt needed to be done.

Now I don't know what to think. What gets me is that I had plenty of opportunity to cheat on her, but I resisted the temptation because I would have felt too guilty about it. Apparently she doesn't care enough about me to feel guilty. She can just jump in bed with whomever happens to come along and feel great about it the next day. I just don't know her anymore.

I strongly believe that a husband and wife should have the freedom to have any friend they want, male or female. My wife and I have discussed that in the past and we agree. When she asked me how I'd feel if she had coffee with her friend Greg, I said, "sure." I didn't think anything of it. It was the worst mistake of my life. I can't believe that she fell in love with him. I trusted her. We had an agreement.

As painful as this is, I still love her and I hope we can work this out. At first I wanted a divorce. But now I am willing to fight to win her back, even though I'm not sure she's worth fighting for. She cheated on me! Maybe I should just end all of this now and get a divorce.

Most betrayed spouses I have counseled are blindsided by the affair. They trusted their spouse and their spouse betrayed that trust. Their feelings swing from wanting a divorce and ending all the misery to wanting to save the marriage at all costs.

The emotional impact of an affair on a betrayed spouse is incredibly powerful. Many cannot sleep for days and experience the worst depression of their lives. At the same time, they are on the verge of angry outbursts, losing their temper whenever they get on the subject of the affair. Their anxiety is also out of control as they panic over where this affair will lead. They see no hope of recovery, their lives totally ruined.

> *The emotional impact of an affair on a betrayed spouse is incredibly powerful.*

The betrayed spouse feels pushed into a pit, crying out for help. The wayward spouse comes to the edge of the pit but instead of tossing a rope, hurls stones. Emotionally torn to pieces, the betrayed spouse can't imagine ever trusting anyone else again, least of all the wayward spouse.

Greg's Side of the Story

There is one other person who is an important part of this drama— the lover. He has a very different perspective on the affair than either Sue or Jon. This is what Greg told me about his affair with Sue.

My friendship with Sue began very innocently. We worked together on a lake restoration project, and that gave us a chance to get to know each other. I was very attracted to her from the first time I laid eyes on her but I knew she was married and I don't believe in interfering with someone else's marriage. So I was very careful not to make any moves that she would interpret as inappropriate.

But as we talked about our personal lives, I about my ex-wife and she about her marriage to Jon, we found many similarities. My ex-wife had ignored me for years and had pursued a career that may have satisfied her, but it sure didn't take me or our kids into account. One day she announced that she was leaving me because she was no longer in love. In the end, she not only left me, but left the kids as well. Now that I look back on my marriage, I'm glad she left because I don't think she ever was in love with me.

Sue's husband had not left her but he may as well have left. He spent very little time with her or the children. All he did was pay the bills. Sue craved attention, and I was willing to give her that attention because I was her friend. I was willing to do the things for her that her husband should have been doing. I helped her with her children, I was there to talk to her whenever she needed to talk, and as our relationship developed, I was able to give her the love and affection that she had been missing in her marriage. I gave her the very things that I had missed in my marriage. And Sue was VERY grateful.

Our friendship is very real and very right. We are two friends who support each other through good times and bad times. We do for each other what a husband and wife should do—we care for each other.

I don't believe that I am the cause of Sue's marriage breaking up. I think Jon is fully to blame for that. She would be making a big mistake not to leave him because, after the dust settles, he'll go right back to working all the time and leaving her home alone.

Sue and I were meant to be together, and I will wait patiently for Sue's divorce. She is not certain what she wants just yet, but I know she loves me and eventually we will be together.

It would be easy to see Greg as the villain in this tragic story. After all, he was the one who pursued a married woman with children. And yet his motives were not entirely selfish. Greg helped Sue as one friend would help another. In fact he did such a good job helping her that she fell in love with him. As the relationship deepened, he became aware of her loveless marriage. After all, that's how Sue described her marriage to Jon—loveless. So, as a friend, he tried to help her with this problem. Greg's own divorce had led him to believe that people sometimes make bad choices when they marry. He saw his divorce as inevitable. So it made sense to conclude that Sue's marriage was also the result of poor judgment. Sue and Jon were simply wrong for each other, and the sooner Sue left her marriage, the happier she would be.

Jon, Sue, and Greg were surprised by what had happened. But if they had understood how vulnerable people are and how easy it is to fall in love with a good friend of the opposite sex, they all would have predicted Sue and Greg's affair.

The Affairs Continuum

Sue's love for Greg made their affair particularly threatening to her marriage. But affairs do not necessarily lead to love. In fact most affairs never do reach the level of emotional attachment that Sue and Greg felt for each other. Why, then, would I select Sue's affair as my main illustration when it is not the most common type?

I have chosen Sue's affair as my primary example because her type of affair makes marital reconciliation seem particularly hopeless. By Sue's own admission, she would have been willing to give up everything in her life for Greg, especially her marriage to Jon. With that attitude, is there anything that can be done to save her marriage? Remarkably, there is a way to achieve that important objective. And that method for recovery works even better in affairs with less emotional attachment.

Since the affair you are struggling with may not be like Sue's affair, it would be helpful for you to see your type of affair in comparison with others. So I will break away from Sue's affair to introduce a variety of ways that people have affairs. The best way for me to describe them is to show you a continuum that reflects the degree of emotional attachment in each affair. On one end of the continuum are affairs like Sue's with intense emotional attachment—those involved consider themselves to be soul mates. But on the other end of the continuum are affairs with almost no attachment at all. The affair you confront probably falls somewhere between these two extemes.

Affairs Continuum

One-Night Stand		Soul Mates
Almost no emotional attachment	Moderate emotional attachment	Intense emotional attachment

The One-Night Stand

On the end of the affair continuum where there is almost no emotional attachment, the "one-night stand" is the most common example. It often takes place when a spouse is away on a trip, or when one has gone out partying without the other spouse. In many cases alcohol is a necessary ingredient for these affairs and it enables people to lose enough of their inhibitions to enjoy sex with a total stranger, or at least someone they don't love. Alcoholics are likely to have many of these loveless affairs during their lifetime. In many cases, they can't even remember who was with them for the night.

"If you're not with the one you love, love the one you're with," is the guiding principle in these affairs. People often begin these short-term relationships in such places as bars and dance clubs. But they can also take place on the job, particularly when a spouse is on a business trip. What begins as a casual working friendship in the morning can end with being in bed together at night.

Many people engaged in short-term relationships become very professional at creating just the right climate for a brief affair. Drinking and dancing usually create the mood, and instinct takes over from there. Both people who participate in a relationship like this usually understand that after the evening is over, there should be no serious effort to build the relationship any further. But a "black book" is usually kept so that a call can be made when it's convenient and the other person might be available for a repeat performance. This happens, not because of an emotional attachment, but because it's easier to get together with someone who already knows you than with a total stranger.

> *While a one-night stand can be an isolated mistake in an otherwise affair-free marriage, it is more often a habit that is repeated by a wayward spouse, sometimes hundreds of times.*

While a one-night stand can be an isolated mistake in an otherwise affair-free marriage, it is more often a habit that is repeated by a wayward spouse, sometimes hundreds of times. Once in a while a one-night stand will develop into a deeper relationship, but that's unusual.

Those most likely to engage in one-night stands are people who travel as part of their job—interstate truck drivers, airline pilots, flight attendants, traveling sales representatives, business consultants, actors, musicians, seminar speakers. The advantage to these short-term flings, from the wayward spouse's perspective, is that they meet a momentary need with no further commitment or consequences.

There are other types of emotionless affairs besides one-night stands. A spouse who hires a prostitute is an example, although even relationships with prostitutes can become emotional. Occasionally, people may have a lengthy affair but never form an emotional attachment to the lover. These people usually have a character disorder that makes it difficult for them to be emotionally attached to anyone.

People who derive a great deal of pleasure from flirting may also have emotionless affairs. Their challenge is to attract someone of the opposite sex. They may not intend the flirting to lead to lovemaking; they may just want to see a willingness to make love, proving their ability to attract a lover. If the flirting leads to sex, that usually ends the relationship. Then the flirt moves on to someone else.

Soul Mates

At the opposite end of the affair continuum are relationships in which there is an intense emotional bond. They usually begin as a friendship, with no flirting whatsoever, and certainly not a one-night stand. Over time the friendship becomes increasingly caring as the partners come to understand each other's emotional needs and learn to meet them. As more and more needs are met with increasing effectiveness, this relationship often becomes so exclusive that it cannot be maintained along with a marriage. Those who separate from their spouse just to "sort things out" are often engaged in this type of affair, unknown to the spouse. The separation allows for the private and exclusive relationship the lovers desire.

Sue and Greg's affair falls into this category of intense emotional bonding. Their friendship began because of their common interests but developed into a mutual ability to meet each other's emotional needs. They did such a good job caring for each other that they had developed an emotional attachment well before they had made love for the first time, so sex was not a primary motivation for their relationship. But once they began making love, it definitely contributed to their becoming soul mates.

Since friendships are the basis of soul mate relationships, it's important to understand how these friendships usually begin. In many cases, a man and woman simply find themselves together because of employment or a special interest. Sometimes they are neighbors or attend the same church.

Simply being together, however, does not create a friendship. A friendship develops from a special willingness to care for each other. When one needs help, the other is there to provide it. In many cases a friendship develops over time as a mutual willingness to help each other unfolds.

> *A friendship develops from a special willingness to care for each other.*

When Greg first joined the Lake Restoration Committee, he needed help understanding some of the issues that were being introduced. Sue met with him after the meetings to answer his questions. They quickly discovered that they held similar views on most issues, and when the committee discussed and then voted on various questions, Greg and Sue could count on each other to support their position.

Greg and Sue's mutual support with committee matters expanded to helping each other with other difficulties they both faced, such as raising children. Their conversations were filled with concern for each other and appreciation for each other's care.

This willingness to help each other created a very deep friendship that existed before either Sue or Greg talked about their feelings for each other. But one night, while they were talking to each other on the telephone, Greg brought up a subject that changed the course of their relationship. He told Sue that he was in love with her. Sue responded that she felt the same way toward him but she didn't want to do anything to threaten her marriage. Unfortunately, it was too late. Their friendship was already threatening her marriage.

A friendship develops into an affair the moment a man and woman feel love for each other and express that love to each other. It opens Pandora's box, and from that point on, neither person seems to have much control over the future of their relationship. Their growing willingness and ability to care for each other creates a growing emotional dependence. They both come to need each other's care so much that an end to their friendship is unthinkable.

It was several weeks after Greg's expression of love that they actually made love. Sue was very reluctant to have sex with Greg. She had told herself that friendship with him was okay, as long as it was platonic. She believed she should be able to have as many friendships with men as she wanted, as long as they were not sexual. But she became increasingly affectionate with Greg, and soon they openly expressed to each other their sexual feelings. Finally, the temptation became too great. Her first sexual experience with him was the most intense and fulfilling she could have ever imagined. In comparison, her sexual relationship with Jon was a joke.

But Sue's affair was no joke, and she knew it. She did not want a divorce because Jon and her children didn't deserve it. She appreciated Jon's ambition and success in his career and she knew how much he loved her. She was also afraid that a divorce might tear her children apart emotionally. Most of the time she convinced herself that as long as no one knew about her affair, no one would ever be hurt. But occasionally the fog of her illusion lifted and she saw the tragedy of what she was doing. In those moments of clarity, she often felt so distraught that she considered suicide.

Most affairs like Sue and Greg's begin as friendships. As the friendship grows, out of genuine concern they try to meet each other's needs. When the needs are met, love is created. Then, one tells the other about his or her feelings of love, the other reveals the same feeling of attraction, and the affair is off and running.

Between One-Night Stands and Soul Mates

I have described the opposite ends of my affairs continuum. One-night stands usually involve little or no emotional attachment while soul mates are highly attached to each other. In between these two poles of my continuum lie the majority of affairs, involving various degrees of emotional attachment.

I have deliberately chosen Sue's affair as my reference example because the soul mate category of affairs seems to make survival of a marriage the most hopeless. As I will explain later, marital recovery requires a complete separation of the wayward spouse and the lover, and the separation of soul mates is quite a challenge. I won't ignore one-night stands and affairs with less attachment than those of soul mates, but those who engage in them are usually willing to end the relationship without much fuss.

However, whether an affair is a one-night stand, years of intimate friendship, or anything in between, the way to end the affair and restore a marriage is essentially the same. So even though my examples throughout this book relate to the affairs of soul mates, the methods I suggest for ending an affair and restoring the marriage can be applied to all affairs.

How Do Affairs Begin?

*S**ue, how could you do this to me?*** Jon's vision of Sue in bed with Greg was indelibly etched in his mind. He could not stop thinking about it and wanting to talk about it. *What did I do to you that would cause you to hurt me so much?*

At first, Sue tried to shut him up by telling him that her relationship with Greg was over, and that they should stop talking about the past. Jon desperately wanted to believe her. She made love to him almost every night for the first week in an attempt to prove that her affair was over and that she was in love with Jon. In an effort to give a convincing performance, she imagined that it was Greg in her arms.

Jon had asked good questions and he desperately needed good answers. Why did Sue have an affair? How did it ever get started? What are the conditions that set these disastrous events into motion, and once in motion why do they usually spin out of control?

How Could It Happen?

We begin our search for answers to these important questions by looking more closely at the players in this drama—Jon, Sue, and

Greg. Each of them helped create the conditions that made the affair possible.

Jon's contribution was his failure to meet Sue's emotional needs. He worked long hours away from her and their children because he felt he was building a secure future for them. He didn't realize that his failure made Sue vulnerable to the first caring man to come into her life.

Sue's contribution was her failure to be honest. She did not tell Jon about her loss of passion for him and she was also dishonest about her developing passion for Greg. Her emotions warned her of the disaster that was to come, but she failed to pass that warning on to Jon.

Greg contributed to the affair by befriending a married woman. At first, he didn't intend to have an affair with Sue. He simply wanted to help her with her problems. His care for her seemed sensible and completely harmless. But his meeting the emotional needs that Jon had failed to meet caused Sue to fall in love with him.

Affairs meet important emotional needs. That's why, despite the suffering experienced by everyone involved, people become ensnared by them. And emotional needs are so powerful that whoever meets them can become irresistible.

What Are Emotional Needs?

An emotional need is a craving that, when satisfied, leaves you with a feeling of happiness and contentment and when unsatisfied, leaves you with a feeling of unhappiness and frustration. There are probably thousands of emotional needs—a need for parties, chocolate, football on TV, shopping—I could go on and on. Each of us has some of these needs and not others. But there are only a very few emotional needs that, when met by someone of the opposite sex, make us so happy that we risk having an affair with that person. I call those our *most important emotional needs*. Those are the ones that make us feel the happiest and most satisfied whenever they are met.

When a husband and wife come to me for help, I first identify their most important emotional needs—what makes each of them feel the best? Then I help them learn to meet those emotional needs for each other. If they learn to do it, they create a fulfilling marriage.

By privately discussing emotional needs with hundreds of men and women, I have discovered that there are ten emotional needs that are usually near the top of the list for most people: the need for admiration, affection, conversation, domestic support, family commitment, financial support, honesty and openness, physical attractiveness, recreational companionship, and sexual fulfillment. (See chapter 8 and appendix A for more information on these needs.)

> Our most important emotional needs are those that make us feel the happiest and most satisfied whenever they are met.

I have also made a revolutionary discovery that has helped me understand why it is so difficult for men and women to meet each other's needs. Whenever I ask couples to list these ten needs according to their priority, men list them one way and women the opposite way. The five emotional needs that men usually place at the top of their list are usually at the bottom of the list for women, and vice versa—the five *most important* emotional needs of women are usually the *least important* of men.

What an insight! No wonder men and women have so much difficulty meeting each other's needs! They are unable to empathize with each other. They feel like doing for each other what *they* would appreciate the most, but it turns out that their efforts are misdirected. What one spouse appreciates the most, the other usually appreciates the least!

Of course, everyone is somewhat unique. While men on average pick a particular five emotional needs and women on average pick the other five, any specific man or woman may pick other combinations. Therefore, I always encourage each spouse to decide what he or she appreciates the most. I never tell people what their emotional needs are. They always tell me. And when those particular needs are met, they will be in love with the one who meets them.

Jon's ambition and his desire to build an attractive lifestyle for his family was not the cause of Sue's affair. The reason Sue was tempted to have an affair was that her most important emotional needs were not considered when Jon made his vocational decisions. He didn't understand how important it was to meet Sue's needs for conversation, affection, and family commitment. By focusing all of his attention on meeting her need for financial support and ignoring her other needs, he left her vulnerable to someone who would meet those other needs. Out of ignorance, he made decisions to achieve their financial objectives at Sue's emotional expense. If he had known how important it was for him to meet Sue's most important emotional needs as he tried to achieve his lifestyle objectives, he would not have had to suffer the pain of her affair.

> *When our most important emotional needs go unmet, we tend to feel somewhat empty and depressed.*

When our most important emotional needs go unmet, we tend to feel somewhat empty and depressed. When those needs are met, we feel alive again—fulfilled. While we all may go through life with unmet emotional needs, none of us is very happy with that kind of life. People who feel depressed because of unmet emotional needs may see therapist after therapist in an effort to relieve their feeling of hopelessness, but they find no relief. They take medication to treat their depression, but that only helps relieve the suffering as long as the medication is used. These people often conclude that there's something wrong with them, that their brain is out of whack, that they are psychologically unstable.

But then they meet someone who makes them feel wonderful. It's as if the clouds have lifted and the sun is shining again. This person usually satisfies the unmet emotional needs quite innocently. It may be that the person is genuinely interested in conversation, expresses admiration that is sincere, or provides exciting companionship. When the unmet emotional needs are fulfilled, the results are incredible. The depressed person is instantly cured—as long as he or she continues to have emotional needs met. When those needs are no longer met, the depression returns.

Some people believe that the lifting of their depression during an affair is a sign from God that they should abandon past relationships and cling to this new relationship. But it's no sign from God. Instead, it's the way our emotions blindly encourage us to spend more time with those who do the best job meeting our emotional needs. If we were to give in to our emotions and chase after anyone who happens to meet our emotional needs at the moment, our lives and the lives of our families would be chaotic in no time. It's very foolish to let our emotions dictate the course of our lives. But unmet needs have a powerful effect—so powerful that people are willing to give up their spouse as well as their children, career, and beliefs to have their emotional needs met.

> *The power of unmet emotional needs explains why people are willing to give up their spouse as well as their children, career, and beliefs to have their emotional needs met.*

To show you how unmet emotional needs lead to an affair, I'll let Sue continue to explain her predicament to you, the same way she explained it to me.

I'm in a relationship with Greg because I've had serious problems with my marriage, only I didn't fully realize it until now. I have been very unhappy with Jon as a husband, and knowing Greg has made that very clear to me. I used to think I had a good marriage, but that was because I never knew what a romantic relationship could be.

Greg and I became good friends very innocently. I was not looking for a replacement for Jon, but my friendship with Greg has shown me what I've been missing all these years. I feel I have turned a critical corner. Greg doesn't earn as much money as Jon but he is very smart and creative and organized, a loving father to his children, and a fun person to hang out with. He's not as good looking as Jon, but I find him more attractive anyway.

Greg and I had worked together on our committee for months without any thoughts of a romantic relationship. When we first met, I never would have guessed in a million years that I would some day be in love with him. But one day we both realized that we felt something for each other.

Greg makes me weak with desire, something I haven't felt in years. We actually talk and look at each other. It seems so natural, like the right thing to do. When we make love it's like heaven. We see each other several times a week but we must be very careful now that Jon knows about us. We joke and laugh and even have very deep conversations about my marriage problems.

Feeling such pleasure and enjoyment from just his company, let alone the intense passion I feel kissing him, makes me realize just how little I was getting from my marriage. I don't want to ruin my kids' lives. They would resent me forever. But I can't lose Greg either. How would I ever be able to find someone else like him?

There are many things about Jon that I admire. In many ways, he's a great guy. I just don't love him. There's no way that he will ever be what I need in a man.

Affairs Satisfy Unmet Emotional Needs

Regardless of where an affair falls on the affairs continuum, it exists because it meets important emotional needs. The one-night stand meets emotional needs when one spouse is temporarily separated from the other spouse. And the one on a trip is not the only one vulnerable—the one who is left alone is also likely to have an affair. When these spouses are separated and, therefore, have unmet emotional needs, they will often find someone else to meet them.

> *Regardless of where an affair falls on the affairs continuum, it exists because it meets important emotional needs.*

The spouses of those who engage in one-night stands are often doing a fairly good job meeting emotional needs when the wayward spouse is home. But when the spouse is not at home, the needs cannot be met. The betrayed spouse may trust the wayward spouse to be faithful because they have never honestly discussed the temptations that exist.

The soul mate type of affair can begin when a spouse works long hours or is often away on business trips. But these affairs can also begin because a spouse fails to meet important emotional needs even when at home. In Jon's case, part of the problem was that he did not spend much time at home, and another part was that when he was at home, he was too tired to meet Sue's emotional needs.

I'm not saying that a betrayed spouse is totally to blame for an affair. I'm simply acknowledging the fact that unmet emotional needs make a spouse vulnerable to the temptation of an affair. In many cases, a person's failure to meet his or her spouse's emotional needs is unintentional.

Jon failed to meet Sue's emotional needs because he did not understand how important they were to her. He was putting all of his energy into a career that he thought would make their whole family happy. He was usually too exhausted when he got home from work to meet Sue's emotional needs for conversation and affection. Because these were important needs that were left unmet, Sue was vulnerable to Greg, who was able to meet needs that Jon did not.

Love, a Powerful Emotion

Unmet emotional needs provide the necessary conditions to set an affair into motion. But what really complicates the situation is the way we can be affected by those who meet our most important emotional needs—we may fall in love. And it's the feeling of love that usually causes affairs to spin out of control.

Right after Jon discovered Sue's affair, Sue was willing to give up her relationship with Greg and she tried to avoid seeing or talking to him. She even gave up her position on the Lake Restoration Committee to get him completely out of her life. But her emotional attachment to him was very strong. All she could think about was being with Greg. She missed the way he met her important emotional needs, but there was more to it than that. She was in love with him.

Love is a very powerful emotional reaction. It's love that motivates us to marry someone. And it's love that keeps us happily married. But it's also love that makes ending an affair extremely difficult.

> *Love makes ending an affair extremely difficult.*

Love certainly determined Sue's conduct, especially after her affair was discovered by Jon. When I asked her why she couldn't leave Greg, she answered, *I love him.* Was that it? Was Sue willing to risk her husband's happiness and her children's future simply because she was in love? I'm afraid so. Her love for Greg was all it took to throw her life and the life of her family into chaos.

How did Sue come to love Greg? And why didn't she love Jon anymore? To help explain what creates and destroys the feeling of love, I invented the concept of the Love Bank.

The Love Bank

You and I have within us a Love Bank, and each person we know has an account in it. The Love Bank helps us keep track of the way people treat us. When people do things that make us feel good, "love units" are deposited, and when they do things that make us feel bad, love units are withdrawn.

Suppose someone makes you feel comfortable when you are together. Ka-chink, a love unit is deposited into their account. If you feel good with that person, two love units might be deposited. Feeling *very good* might warrant a three-love-unit deposit. Or if the person does something that makes you feel so good you are likely to remember it for several weeks, four love units might be deposited. You can see how someone who is consistent in making you happy could eventually accumulate quite a large account in your Love Bank. And the higher a person's account is, the more emotionally attracted you are to that person.

But just as people can deposit love units, they can also withdraw them. Someone who makes you feel uncomfortable will withdraw one love unit from their account. If that person makes you feel bad, two love units are withdrawn. Feeling *very bad* results in the loss of three love units. And if you feel so bad you will remember the experience for a while, four love units will disappear from the account. If someone withdraws all the love units he or she ever deposited and then goes on to drive the account deeply into the red, you find you are repulsed by that person.

The feeling of attraction to someone is the way our emotions encourage us to spend time with people who treat us well. When someone makes us happy, our emotions associate that person with happiness, and we want to be with him or her. Similarly, when someone makes us consistently unhappy, our emotions usually tell us to avoid that person.

When a certain threshold in the Love Bank is reached with someone of the opposite sex—say a thousand love units—the emotional reaction we call romantic love is triggered. It's not just *attraction* that we feel, it's *incredible attraction.* We don't simply *like* the person, we are *captivated by* the person. We feel wonderful when we are together and often feel terrible when apart. The feeling of love is unmistakable and overwhelming.

> *The feeling of attraction to someone is the way our emotions encourage us to spend time with people who treat us well.*

As long as your account in someone's Love Bank stays above the romantic love threshold, he or she will be in love with you. So how can a couple keep their Love Bank balances high enough to experience romantic love? By making large deposits regularly. And the best way to do that is to meet each other's emotional needs. Unless couples meet those needs, their love for each other cannot be sustained throughout life.

Unfortunately, when a Love Bank balance drops below the romantic love threshold, a siren does not go off, warning us of the danger. Instead, we simply lose the feeling of love we had for our spouse. This loss of love is usually regarded as the normal settling in of marriage partners to a more mature relationship. But actually it is the beginning of serious trouble.

Jon let his account in Sue's Love Bank fall well below her romantic love threshold. He stopped meeting her emotional needs, and over time, all of the love units he had deposited during their courtship and early marriage drained out. On the other hand, Greg's account in her Love Bank soared well over her romantic love threshold. He met the needs that Jon failed to meet and deposited love units every time he was with Sue. The result was that she loved Greg and didn't love her husband, Jon.

The feeling of love that Sue had for Greg, and her loss of love for Jon, made marital reconciliation very difficult. Greg had a huge emotional edge on Jon. Whenever Sue was with Jon, his low Love Bank balance made her feel uncomfortable, so she really didn't care to be with him that much. On the other hand, Greg's Love Bank balance made her feel terrific. So she looked forward to every moment they could be together.

As long as Greg kept his Love Bank balance high by continuing to meet Sue's emotional needs, Jon's efforts to make Sue happy would pale in comparison. It's very difficult for a person with a depleted Love Bank account to compete with someone with an overflowing account. Jon came to understand his disadvantage all too well in the months ahead.

How Do Affairs Usually End?

S ue's attitude toward Jon would not have given him much hope for their marital reconciliation. But Sue had not told Jon how she felt about him—and how much she loved Greg. Instead, she told Jon that the affair was over and she wanted to be reconciled to him.

I met with Jon for the first time soon after he discovered Sue and Greg in bed with each other. He was devastated and could barely talk to me through his tears.

I found my wife having sex with another man, in our house, in our bed, with our children asleep. After all the crying and all the whys, we had a long talk. She told me how sorry she was for hurting me and how she wanted to be with me for the rest of her life. Some of the reasons she gave me I understood and I was at fault. I can admit my mistakes. These mistakes or errors that I have committed will be addressed and fixed. I do love her with all my heart. In fact sometimes I feel I love her too much.

This hurt, though, is hard to handle. I can forgive her and I think I do forgive her, but my problem is not the forgiving; it's the forgetting. I keep seeing her in bed with the other man. It just pops into my head all the time—there are so many things that make me think about it.

Sue wanted to go away for the weekend, just the two of us. At first I was so excited by the thought of spending the weekend with her. And then I remembered what she looked like in bed with another man. I made up an excuse why we couldn't go.

Last night she wanted to have a dinner at a very romantic restaurant. There was soft music and candlelight. I was enjoying myself for most of the evening; then the vision of her in bed with the other man popped into my head again. I told her I wasn't feeling well and we left. In the car she asked me what was wrong. I couldn't talk about it because I was ready to cry again. I know that I will eventually get through this but I've never been so sad in all my life.

For the betrayed spouse an affair is, without a doubt, one of life's most painful experiences. Jon reacted the way most people react when they discover that their husband or wife has had an affair. The pain seems unbearable. The person you trusted the most hurts you in the worst way possible.

Jon was devastated by what Sue had done. But if he had known Sue's true feelings, he would have been even more upset. Sue was lying to Jon, trying to convince him that things would soon be back to normal again. But in reality, the worst was yet to come.

In the week following the discovery of her affair, Sue did everything she could to convince Jon that their marriage was on track again. In a way, she did want her marriage to work. But Jon's lukewarm response to her efforts, combined with her love for Greg, gave her little hope for recovery, and she became very depressed. To make matters worse, Jon announced that he would be gone for two days on an emergency business trip. He apologized for the timing but claimed he had no control over the decision. Sue felt that she was back to square one, married to a man whose career came first and who would never be able to meet her emotional needs.

The first night that Sue was left alone, she was filled with an overwhelming sense of emptiness, fearing that she was destined to live her life without her soul mate. The more she thought about her hopeless future, the more desperate she became. Finally, she could no longer take it. So she did what she had promised Jon she wouldn't do—she called Greg.

As soon as Greg answered the telephone and she heard his voice, Sue's depression was completely lifted. She felt energized and alive again and knew at once that she could not live without him. Greg had missed her too but told her he didn't want to interfere with her marriage and that their future was up to her. Before the conversation ended, they made plans to see each other again, but this time they had to be more careful.

A Secret Second Life Enables an Affair to Grow

For an affair to continue, it must be kept secret from the unsuspecting spouse. So a secret second life must be created to nurture an affair. When married couples tend to lead independent lives and do not pay much attention to each other, that secret second life is easy to create. But when a husband and wife live a more integrated life, it requires much more deception.

Jon and Sue had quite innocently developed independent lives. Since Jon worked so many hours, Sue had interests, activities, and friends that Jon knew nothing about. She hadn't tried to keep them from him—she often tried to tell him about her day, but he didn't show much interest in her activities. She eventually stopped trying to tell him about them. Then, when her relationship with Greg started to develop, she deliberately left information about him out of her conversations with Jon. She even started to lie about where she was and what she was doing so that Jon would not get suspicious.

Sue actually began lying to Jon about the time she spent with Greg long before the relationship had turned into an affair. Deep down she knew that their friendship was getting out of control but she did not want it to end. When Jon asked about what she had done on a given day, she lied occasionally to avoid telling him that she had been with Greg.

After Jon knew about their affair, Sue and Greg conspired together to deceive him. Sue would park her car at a shopping mall, and Greg would pick her up so that if Jon went looking for her, he wouldn't find her car near Greg's house. Sue made telephone calls to Greg from pay phones, just in case Jon was tapping her home telephone. She called Jon at work just before getting together with Greg to give Jon the impression that she was home alone. Whenever she was with Greg, she created a believable story for Jon.

Often wayward spouses, like Sue, do not have a history of lying, but their affair turns them into masters of deception. Once in a while the fog will lift, and they see how dishonest they have become. When that happens, they usually panic and recognize the affair for the mistake it is. But eventually the fog comes back, clouding their reason, and they go back to their lifestyle of cheating and lying.

> *Wayward spouses do not necessarily have a history of lying, but their affair turns them into masters of deception.*

Throughout their marriage, Sue and Jon had allowed free access to each other's personal information, and that understanding made Sue's effort to deceive Jon very stressful for her. She felt obligated to answer his questions about her whereabouts whenever he asked, and that meant she always had to prepare a lie to explain each time she was with Greg.

Since Jon and Sue had a history of being honest and open with each other, it was not easy for Sue to maintain her secret second life. So she tried to change the way she and Jon related to each other. She no longer wanted to be open with Jon and asked him to respect her privacy.

How to Keep a Second Life Secret

"Stay Out of My Private Life!"

One of the most common clues that an affair is going on is an unfaithful spouse's unwillingness to let the other spouse know about all aspects of his or her life. If a spouse refuses to talk about the events of the day, it may be a sign that a secret second life exists. When an unfaithful spouse makes his or her life a private matter, off-limits to the betrayed spouse's inquiries, the secret second life is difficult to discover.

In an effort to improve honesty and openness, I asked one couple to share with each other their e-mail passwords and access to their voice mail. The husband refused, claiming that everyone should have some privacy in their life. My request was so threatening to him that he stopped meeting with me. I warned his wife, in his presence, that his secrecy could be due to an affair.

To compensate for his unwillingness to continue therapy, he bought his wife flowers on several occasions, made dinner for her, and took her out on a few dates. But eventually, she called to let me know that my hunch was right. She had discovered that her husband was having an affair.

> *Privacy isn't something that improves marriages. It's honesty and openness that improve marriages.*

When you stop to think about it, privacy isn't something that improves marriages. It's honesty and openness that improve marriages. The more information you have about each other's thoughts and activities, the easier it is to meet each other's needs and resolve conflicts. Privacy actually blocks access to that important information, and that ultimately leads to marital failure.

As long as Jon was free to ask Sue about every aspect of her life, deception was a full-time job. She had to concoct a story every time she saw Greg, which was very often. As time went on, she realized that it would be much easier to carry on her secret second life if she didn't have to always account for her whereabouts.

She told Jon that one of the reasons she didn't love him as much as she should was because he violated her right to privacy. He overstepped his boundaries and didn't give her a chance to breathe. She said she would love him much more if he would back off and let her have some privacy, not having to always account for her whereabouts.

Jon didn't buy Sue's argument for privacy. He had already seen evidence of lies, and when she asked for privacy, he suspected that she might be back with Greg.

"I'm Disappointed You Don't Trust Me"

Another way Sue tried to defend her secret second life was to appeal to trust. When Jon raised questions about her suspicious activities, Sue often expressed shock that he could be so distrusting as to even ask these questions. She tried to make it seem as if such questions were incredibly disrespectful. Sue believed that the best defense was a good offense, and so she tried to make Jon feel guilty whenever he asked questions regarding her activities.

One day Jon came right out and asked Sue the obvious question, *Are you still seeing Greg?*

Sue fired back with shock, anger, sarcasm, and sadness, *How can you think that of me after how hard I've worked to get our marriage back together? For all my effort, this is all I get. Unless you can put what I did behind you, I'm afraid we don't have much of a future together.*

Then with righteous indignation, Sue stomped out of the room. She followed it up by not speaking to Jon the rest of the day and she didn't make love to him for a week. Her strategy worked great because it meant she didn't have to pretend that everything was okay between them, and it kept Jon from asking her any more questions about Greg.

The I'm-disappointed-you-don't-trust-me tactic throws the betrayed spouse off balance, making him or her feel guilty and hesitant to pursue the issue. But it kept Jon from asking questions for only about a week. Eventually he saw the strategy for what it was, an effort to protect Sue's secret second life, so he went back to asking questions again.

"I Can't Remember"

Most of us can remember what we did last night. Even if we have to take some time to think of it, we can generally give pretty specific information. And a week later, if we are asked, we are able to provide essentially the same report. But if we were to lie about what we did last night, we would find it surprisingly difficult, a week later, to remember exactly how the lie went.

If I suspect that a client is lying to me, I ask for specific information, and record it carefully. Then I ask again and again, each time recording what the client says. If the person is telling me the truth, each description of the event is essentially the same. But with a lie, the description changes each time it is repeated.

Jon learned to use the same tactic to uncover lies, and eventually Sue knew what he was doing. So she used another common defense: "I can't remember."

When a person is having an affair, he or she often prefers to provide no information about the secret life, lest someone ask for the story to be repeated, or even worse, check it out. I have encouraged many spouses to ask their husband or wife where he or she has been and what he or she was doing. If the response is, "I really can't remember," it sends up a red flag. Of course the person can remember. But being willing to reveal what is remembered is another matter.

As soon as Sue began using her poor memory as a defense, Jon tried to confront her, saying that her memory for events had been very good in the past. But she insisted that her marital problems had been so upsetting to her that her memory was affected.

"We're Just Friends"

It was an innocent discovery on Jon's part. A business associate happened to mention that he had seen Sue that day. With a few questions Jon learned that she was having lunch with a man that fit Greg's description.

> Since many affairs are with friends, it's often difficult to distinguish between an affair and an innocent friendship.

Since many affairs are with friends, it's often difficult to distinguish between an affair and an innocent friendship. Friends and lovers often do the same things—have lunch together, talk on the telephone, send notes, and give each other gifts. A neighbor, a married friend, a coworker, a personal trainer, a professor, a student, a pastor, anyone with whom there is repeated contact and needs are being met, can be a friend—or a lover.

Friends usually meet emotional needs, and love units are deposited when needs are met. So it's easy to understand why friends of the opposite sex would fall in love. Once the friends are in love, the friendship can then be used as an excuse for being together, particularly when there is no hard evidence of an affair.

But in Sue's case, even though Jon had that hard evidence when he found Sue and Greg in bed together, she tried to use the defense that they were just friends.

Jon didn't buy it, of course, and Sue instinctively reverted back to her shock, anger, sarcasm, and sadness. *My affair with Greg is over, but that doesn't mean we can't be friends. Do you expect me to live in a cave all my life?*

Again, with righteous indignation, Sue stomped out of the room, did not speak to Jon the rest of the day, and wouldn't make love to him. But this time her strategy did not work. Jon knew that her affair was on again and he was very angry. After he regained his composure the next day, he demanded, again, that she stop seeing Greg. Sue told him that he was being controlling and paranoid.

"I Just Need Some Time Away to Think Things Through"

Sue had stopped coming with Jon to their appointments with me almost from the start, because she did not like my suggestion that she stop seeing or talking to Greg. But Jon continued to talk to me throughout his ordeal. By this time we both knew that Sue was continuing her affair with Greg, but I encouraged Jon to stick it out, even if they eventually separated. Jon remained hopeful because I predicted that Sue's affair would eventually end, and he would have a chance to reconcile. But I prepared him for the possibility that they might separate first.

When a spouse asks for a separation to "think things through" or to "decide how I feel," I usually interpret this as his or her way of getting together with a lover more conveniently. The reason I jump to this conclusion so quickly is that I have been right so much of the time.

Sue had grown tired of trying to live a life of deception. She knew that Jon was now on to her, and it would be almost impossible to continue seeing Greg without Jon knowing about it. So she began making plans for a separation.

Moving in with Greg was out of the question. For one thing, his house was much too small. Besides, it was one thing for Jon to think she was having an affair, but quite another for him to know about it with certainty.

Asking Jon to leave his home and children was also a problem for

Sue. How could she hurt him that much, when he had done nothing to deserve it? Having an affair was bad enough, but Sue didn't think she could live with herself if she took Jon away from his children.

So she decided to look for an apartment where she would live by herself for a while. From there she could visit her children at home as much as she wanted and she would be free to be with Greg without being under Jon's watchful eye. It seemed like the perfect solution.

After she found a place to live near her home, she waited for Jon's next interrogation, and she didn't have to wait very long. As they were eating dinner as a family, he innocently asked Sue what she had done that day. Sue looked him in the eye and said, *It's none of your business.*

It certainly is my business, Jon responded, and that's all Sue needed.

Sue got up from the table. *I've had just about enough of your jealousy and control. I can't take it anymore.*

Then she announced that she would be moving out the next morning.

Her children were heartbroken. They could not understand why she would leave them, but she promised to come back as soon as she was "feeling better." She told Jon the same thing.

Because I had prepared Jon for this turn of events, he was able to be considerate of her feelings and even help her move. Without such preparation, I'm sure he would have flown into a rage, giving Sue additional justification for her actions. But instead, he told her that he wanted her to be happy and that he hoped the separation would make her feel better about being married to him.

The next day Jon rented a truck and helped her move furniture from the house that would make her apartment comfortable. He even gave her money to cover the cost of the apartment.

Sue had done what she had been dreaming about doing for months—leaving Jon so she could be with Greg. She was free.

As soon as Jon left her apartment, Sue called Greg, inviting him over. This was the day she had planned—moving to her own place and having a private evening with Greg. It was wonderful being with him, but she missed her children terribly. She hadn't expected that, and after Greg left, she cried herself to sleep.

An Affair Is an Illusion

Until her separation, whenever Sue was with Greg, she was almost always happy because he met some of her most important emotional needs. Her conversation with him was enjoyable and interesting, and he always gave her his undivided attention when they talked to each other. He showered her with affection, continually giving her assurance that he loved her and would always be there for her if she needed him. He also had a great sense of humor, another thing missing in her life with Jon.

Sue's relationship with Greg had been essentially free of conflict. They deliberately avoided any unpleasant subjects when they were together. It was as if they were living in a kind of bubble, protected from the cares of normal living. So they rarely argued about anything.

The special world that Sue and Greg had created was designed to maximize their feeling of love. They spent their time together meeting each other's emotional needs and avoiding anything that would upset the other. Love-unit deposits were abundant, and withdrawals were very few. So many love units were deposited that they had left the romantic-love threshold way behind. Their balances were so high that they believed their love for each other would last forever.

But the conditions that had made Sue's affair so enjoyable for her were created at Jon's expense. Sue and Greg had very few conflicts because Jon was shouldering many of the mundane responsibilities of Sue's life. It was his work and his income that gave Sue the quality of life she enjoyed and the freedom to create the conditions that made her affair work. She had her part-time job, child care available to her when she needed it, and the ability to come and go as she pleased.

But her separation changed all that.

With Separation Comes Reality

When Sue was with Greg after she left her family, all was not a bed of roses anymore. She began to doubt whether she had done the right thing. All she could think about was how her children looked at her when she left them. Even Greg could not cheer her up, and that was the beginning of trouble for their relationship. Until then, they always had fun together, but after the separation, it wasn't fun anymore. And that withdrew love units.

The first week Sue spent as much time with Greg as she could. But she discovered almost immediately that having Greg as a lover was very different than having him as a husband. Of course, he wasn't her husband yet, but she began thinking of him in those terms. Being away from Jon helped her realize how much she had depended on him for things she took for granted, and how Greg simply wasn't able to fill his shoes entirely. He would never be able to earn the income that Sue had come to expect and he would never be the real father of her children. Jon and Sue had created a very comfortable lifestyle together, and as she sat in her apartment, she began to miss it terribly.

Before the separation, whenever Sue and Greg talked about their future together, they would imagine how wonderful it would be. But they had never actually worked out the details. Now they were faced with the reality of it all. Now when they tried to plan Sue's divorce, all she could talk about was her guilt and depression. Greg grew impatient with her and love units were withdrawn from both of their Love Banks. Lovemaking just wasn't the same after such conversations.

Sue believed that the way she felt about Greg was a sign that they were meant to be together. She didn't understand that it was Greg's balance in her Love Bank that made her feel the way she did. And the only reason he was able to deposit so many love units was that they had created a lifestyle insulated from the problems of everyday life. But as soon as she left Jon, the bubble was broken.

It wasn't long before Sue's intense feelings of love for Greg began to change. And without her passion for him, she was able to begin to see the reality of her world—a husband who loved her, children who needed her, and a lifestyle that was the envy of everyone she knew. What could she have been thinking?

The fog lifted, and Sue called Jon. He was so glad to hear from her that he could hardly talk. When she asked him how he'd feel if she returned home, he was ecstatic. By the end of the day, she was with her family again. Her return home was a good sign, but I warned Jon that Sue's awakening would probably be short-lived.

Within a week, she was back in her apartment again. She had missed Greg terribly and couldn't stop thinking about him. She had actually talked to him several times by phone, and that was all it took to redeposit many of the love units that had been lost. Once again she was crazy about him, and the illusion of the affair completely possessed her. She couldn't remember the guilt and depression she felt when separated. All she could think about was living the rest of her life with Greg.

But she wasn't back in her apartment a day before the fog lifted again and she saw the mess she was making of her life. The depression she felt was so severe that she started to think about suicide as the only way out of the terrible trap she had created. But instead of killing herself, she made an appointment with a counselor to help her think things through.

Sue had avoided talking to me because she knew I would have encouraged her to leave Greg permanently, something she didn't want to face. So she found another counselor who would agree with her.

Sue's new counselor suggested that her depression was caused by separating from her children. To help her overcome the depression, the counselor encouraged her to ask Jon to leave their home so she could return. She had been resisting that plan because she didn't want to hurt Jon any more than he had already been hurt. But she had become so depressed that in desperation, she took the counselor's advice and asked Jon to leave his home, which he reluctantly agreed to do.

Living at home with her children, however, did not alleviate Sue's depression. In fact her feeling of hopelessness seemed to intensify, so antidepressant medication was prescribed to help her cope with the pain.

Sue saw Greg regularly, but the good feelings she used to have when they were together became increasingly difficult to create. She felt a great deal of guilt and depression in spite of the therapy and the medication she was taking. Greg wanted her to file for divorce and marry him, but Sue resisted the idea. Deep down she knew that he was not what she wanted as a husband. He was great in the insulated bubble they had created during their affair, but in the real world, she saw huge problems on the horizon. Her children were very unhappy about the prospect of her divorce, and she knew that Greg would never be able to provide the standard of living she had come to enjoy. Already, when she had tried to get financial help from Greg, she found that he was not the generous man she had known when she didn't need much. They started fighting with each other for the first time, and it was about money.

Money wasn't their only conflict, though. There were many issues that seemed to pop out of nowhere. For example, the care of their children became a point of contention. During their affair, they tended to ignore their children when they were together so that they could give each other undivided attention. But now they found themselves ignoring each other when they were with the children. Their time together was no longer insulated and carefree. Instead, they spent their time trying to address the real problems that Sue's separation had created.

I knew that Sue would eventually lose her love for Greg if they spent time together in the real world instead of in their protective bubble. Greg really didn't have what it took to make a good husband for Sue, because he lacked the ability to meet some of the needs that Jon had been meeting. On the other hand, I felt that Jon could meet the needs that Greg had met, if Sue would give him a chance. Sue's feeling of love for Greg maintained her illusion that they would be great together. But they were really not that compatible, and living in the real world revealed this to her.

I was not sure that Sue would see the light quickly enough for her marriage to be saved. Her behavior took a great toll on her account in Jon's Love Bank. All of the love units she had deposited over the years of their marriage together were cascading out of his bank. Each time I spoke with him, he was becoming increasingly disinterested in saving the marriage, and he even wondered if he loved her anymore.

But before the year had ended, Sue and Jon's relationship got the break it needed. Sue discovered that Greg had developed a friendship with another woman. Up to that moment, Sue was very confused. She loved Greg, but couldn't imagine marrying him. That perpetual state of stress left her an emotional basket case, but she couldn't let go.

When she found out that Greg was cheating on *her,* however, the light dawned. It made a lot of sense to her that a man who was willing to have an affair with her would also be willing to cheat on her. Greg was no longer the knight in shining armor that she had loved and respected. After a fight to end all fights, where she called him every name in the book, and he responded by telling her that he had never thought much of her either, their relationship finally came to an end. Greg told Sue that he was in love with the other woman, someone without a husband or children, and he encouraged Sue to return to her husband.

Even after all that, Greg's leaving was devastating to Sue. She cried, begged him to reconsider, and threatened suicide. But too many love units had been withdrawn already, and he had lost his love for her. Her desperation withdrew even more, and it was hard for him to remember what he had ever seen in her.

Immediately after her fight with Greg, Sue, in desperation, called Jon and invited him to return home to her. He had been waiting months for that invitation and knew how to respond. He graciously accepted.

As soon as Jon moved back to their home, he found Sue to be as depressed as he had ever seen her. She slept all day and could hardly eat anything. The entire experience had just about destroyed her.

> ## Most affairs die a natural death.

At some point, most affairs die a natural death. In some cases, it's the lover who ends the relationship, finding that the wayward spouse isn't living up to expectations. And in other cases, it's the wayward spouse who ends it, when the disadvantages of the affair begin to outweigh the advantages. Regardless of who ends the affair, it usually happens when the affair becomes more trouble than it's worth.

Occasionally a scorned lover will go berserk, call all hours of the day and night, file lawsuits, and create all kinds of trouble. But that's very rare. Affairs usually end quietly.

The vast majority of affairs, especially one-night stands and other affairs with low emotional attachment, are kept secret and never revealed to spouses. This is true even when children are born of an affair and a betrayed husband unwittingly raises a child he thinks is his.

Because affairs are based on dishonesty and thoughtlessness, they rarely survive. The same self-centeredness that creates an affair is also responsible for its destruction, because no relationship can survive long without honesty and consideration.

How Should Affairs End?

Sue's affair with Greg ended the way most affairs end—it died a natural death. Once an affair is exposed to the realities of life, the protective bubble usually breaks and the passion fades away. Without passion, the stupidity of an affair becomes painfully apparent to everyone involved, and the only emotion left is depression of the worst kind.

The affair was bad enough for Jon, but the way it ended seemed even worse. Greg left Sue. Only then was she willing to have Jon come back home. Jon had won her back only because Greg was no longer interested in her. If I had not prepared him for this likely outcome, I doubt that Jon would have been willing to give his marriage another chance.

I have already given you a glimpse of what my advice to Sue was when I saw her immediately after she and Greg were discovered together. I simply suggested that she never see or talk to Greg again. She did try to follow my advice for about a week, but her attachment to Greg ultimately got the best of her.

However, there are couples who have followed my advice. They were spared the pain and suffering that Sue and Jon endured in the months following the exposure of her affair. And their marital recovery was much easier because they ended their affair the right way.

How *should* an affair end? Lee and Kevin's experience is a good example of how it should be done.

Kevin and Lee's Story

Hey Kevin, what's up? As Kevin's friend and coworker, Amy knew something was wrong.

Oh, it's nothing, probably just the forty thing, Kevin responded, referring to the fact that he had just turned forty. He had a great job as manager of an auto dealership, and had four beautiful children. But he was unhappy with the way his life was turning out.

His discontent was with his wife, Lee. She had changed, and Kevin wasn't sure why. She had always been there for him, with encouraging conversation and affection that seemed to have no limits. Lee had also looked sensational, and they used to have a wonderful sex life together. Unfortunately these were all just memories.

Kevin noticed a change in Lee when their first child was born. He knew that children would require adjustments in their lifestyle, but he never thought that a child would create such a transformation in Lee's attitude toward him. Before their child arrived, Kevin seemed to be her highest priority in life, but after the child, he seemed to be her lowest priority.

Their second child made matters even worse. All the love and affection that Lee had given to Kevin during the first years of their marriage were now refocused on their two children. As two more children arrived, Kevin and Lee's relationship continued to deteriorate.

Lee was a good mother and gave her children excellent care. She kept them clean and well fed, helped them with homework, and was their chauffeur to music lessons, sports practice, and church events. But her self-sacrificing care for the children kept her in a constant state of exhaustion. She knew something was lacking in her relationship with Kevin but she was simply too busy and too tired to give it much thought, let alone do something about it.

Amy knew that Kevin hadn't been his happy-go-lucky self for some time and she was concerned about him. *You seem to be really down about something, Kevin. I'm a good listener,* Amy said, encouraging him to confide in her.

In the next two hours, Kevin poured his heart out. Nearly in tears, he explained how depressed he had been lately. He just didn't feel like doing much of anything anymore, and had little enthusiasm for life. He also mentioned how his relationship with Lee had suffered over the years—how low he was on her list of priorities.

Amy listened attentively. Trying to help, she suggested that he might start an exercise program with Lee as a way of rebuilding their relationship and his health, all at the same time. *I started working out at the health club last month. It sure has made me feel better. I could get you two free passes if you'd like.*

Wow! Kevin thought. *That does sound like a good idea. Maybe that's all Lee and I need—a little time together.*

That night Kevin told Lee about the passes and suggested they plan to go out together at least twice a week. But Lee did not share his enthusiasm. *I really wouldn't want to leave the children alone at night. But it might not be a bad idea for you to go. It might make you feel a little better if you got some exercise.*

So Kevin decided to work out twice a week—with Amy. The exercise made him feel much better, and it wasn't long before he increased it to three times a week, then four, and finally he met Amy almost every day. He lost fifteen pounds, built endurance and muscle tone, and had not felt so good in years. Each morning he could hardly wait to meet Amy for their morning workout.

Lee encouraged Kevin to go to the health club every morning, because she could see how much healthier and happier he had become. But she didn't realize that Amy was exercising with Kevin. It wasn't that Kevin had lied about it—the topic of his exercise partner simply never came up.

It wasn't long before Kevin and Amy had fallen in love with each other. It was predictable, because they spent the most enjoyable moments of each day together. They were both able to conceal their emotions fairly well at first. But it was only a matter of time before the truth was revealed.

One day when they were together, Kevin brought up the subject of Amy's husband, Al. It was quite an innocent question: *How is Al doing these days?*

Amy became very quiet. Suddenly tears streamed down her face. When she regained her composure, she told Kevin for the first time what a bitter disappointment Al had been to her. She had always hoped to have children and raise a family, but from the time they were married, he had been unable to keep a job and was unemployed most of the time. It was up to Amy to pay most of the bills. If that wasn't bad enough, to entertain himself he spent most of his time with friends who had as little ambition as he had. When Amy came home from work, he was usually nowhere to be found. She had lost her love for him and had already seen an attorney to file for divorce.

Kevin gave her a hug as she cried. Amy hugged him back and then gave him a kiss. Their kiss expressed what they had been secretly feeling for each other for weeks. Neither of them wanted it to stop.

When Kevin returned home, Lee could see that something was wrong. He seemed very aloof. That was unusual. He was almost always cheerful and talkative, playing with the kids and chatting with her. Tonight he had nothing to say.

Lee was alarmed by the sudden change in Kevin's mood, and wanted to know what it was all about. At first, Kevin tried to lie to her, saying that it had been a disappointing day at work. But Lee knew that disappointing days didn't affect Kevin that way. He was able to leave his work behind him. So she pressed on and kept asking him questions about what had happened that day to upset him so much. Finally, he admitted to her that he was in love with another woman.

Lee was stunned and then became angry. But she was able to compose herself and, as calmly as possible, she asked Kevin to tell her all about it. Reluctantly, he did. He explained how unhappy he had been in their marriage and how Amy had become someone who really seemed to care about him. She had become his best friend, and now he was in love with her.

I was able to talk to both Kevin and Lee the next day. During our session together, they explained the circumstances that led them to my office, and then I pointed out what had not yet happened to them—Kevin had not yet made love to Amy. He had not yet created a secret second life to give himself greater opportunity to be with her. He had not yet decided to separate from Lee and his children. He had not yet found that Amy wasn't really the woman he wanted after all. And he had not yet begged an extremely resentful Lee to give him another chance after almost destroying her life. So far, he had not acted on his love for another woman. Kevin knew that if he stopped his relationship with Amy now, he could avoid all the tragic events that accompany a full-blown affair.

The conditions that Kevin had allowed himself to experience just about guaranteed that he would fall in love with Amy. She had become his best friend, and they were spending the best moments of the day with each other. It's the formula for the creation of love.

The feeling of love is one of the most powerful emotions we ever experience, and it's very difficult to leave someone you love. Yet that's exactly what Kevin had to do and he had to do it immediately.

Total Separation—The Right Way to End an Affair

Although Kevin was in no position to bargain, he tried anyway. Like others in his position, he tried to keep Amy in the loop somehow. You'd think that a wayward spouse would be so aware of his or her weakness and so aware of the pain inflicted that he or she would be thoughtful enough to make every effort to avoid further contact with the lover. Instead, the wayward spouse often argues that the relationship was "only sexual" or was "only emotional, but not sexual" or some other peculiar description to prove that continued contact with the lover would be okay. In Kevin's case, it was "only emotional."

Most betrayed spouses intuitively understand the danger and demand that all contact with a lover end for life. Permanent separation not only helps prevent a renewal of the affair, but it is also a crucial gesture of consideration to the betrayed spouse.

> *Permanent separation not only helps prevent a renewal of the affair, but it is also a crucial gesture of consideration to the betrayed spouse.*

In spite of career sacrifices, friendships, and issues relating to children's schooling, I recommend with all seriousness that there be a sudden and complete end to an affair. And I recommend extreme measures to ensure total separation for life from a former lover.

The Addictive Power of an Affair

Several years ago, I owned and operated ten chemical dependency treatment clinics. At first, we used several different treatment strategies. For some, we tried to encourage moderation, and for others, we tried to achieve total abstinence. It wasn't long before all the counselors agreed that total abstinence was the only way to save drug or alcohol addicts from their self-destructive behavior. Unless they completely abandoned the object of their addiction, the addiction usually returned. For these people, moderation was impossible. The conviction that their drug of choice was off-limits to them for life helped end their cycle of addiction-treatment-addiction.

My strategy for ending an affair with total separation from the lover developed after my experience treating addicts. And, over the years, I've found my total-separation strategy to be very effective in ending affairs in a way that makes marital recovery possible. Without total separation, marital recovery is almost impossible.

> *Without total separation, marital recovery is almost impossible.*

An affair is a very powerful addiction. The craving to be with the lover can be so intense that objective reality doesn't have much of a chance. The fact that a spouse and children may be permanently injured by this cruel indulgence doesn't seem to matter. All that matters is spending more time with the lover. That makes it an addiction.

Even the one-night stand may be an addiction. It may not be an addiction to a particular lover, but it may still be an addiction—to one-night stands. In affairs that have low emotional attachment, the addiction is often to the act of having sex itself, rather than to a particular lover.

The addiction to one-night stands can also grow from a need to be continually assured of one's attractiveness. People who indulge in such practices want to feel that they can have anyone they want, even that person over there sitting at the bar. These people who need constant reassurance of their attractiveness must learn some other way to gain that assurance—a way that does not destroy their marriage.

The analogy between chemical addiction and an affair is striking. In both cases, the first step toward recovery is admitting that the addiction is self-destructive and harmful to those whom the addict cares for the most—his or her family. After recognizing the need to overcome the addiction, the next step is to suffer through the symptoms of withdrawal. Addicts are often admitted to a hospital or treatment program during the first few weeks of withdrawal to ensure total separation from the addicting substance.

The way to overcome an addiction is tried and proven—abstain from the object of addiction. Alcoholics, for example, must completely avoid contact with any alcoholic beverage to gain control over their addictive behavior. They must avoid places where alcohol is likely to be found, such as bars and parties. They must even avoid friends who drink occasionally in their presence. They must surround themselves with an alcohol-free environment. In the same way, when a wayward spouse separates from the lover, extraordinary precautions must be taken to avoid all contact with the lover—for life.

Of course, my advice is not easy to implement. Many people who have had an affair try but fail to make a drastic and decisive break with their lover. In the case of Sue and Jon, Sue managed to be separated from Greg for about a week but couldn't resist talking to him. So her affair continued until it finally died a natural death, leaving pain and suffering in its wake.

But while total separation is not easy to implement, there are ways to make it work. I helped Kevin and Lee create such a plan.

How to Tell a Lover That the Relationship Is Over

How can I explain to Amy that I will never see her again? Kevin asked. The answer to that question is an extremely important part of the plan to separate. Kevin needed to end the relationship in a way that would make their separation complete. And he also needed to do it in a way that would be least offensive to Lee.

But Kevin's instincts would not have led him to the correct procedure. If left to his own devices, he would have taken Amy on a Caribbean cruise to say their final good-byes. At the very least, he would have wanted to take her to a secluded spot and discuss the pros and cons of their future together. From Kevin's perspective, he would want to let her down gently, and end the relationship with care and concern for her future. After all, he had encouraged her to love him, and now he felt he had no right to abandon her with no warning. Besides, he wasn't just in love with her, he cared about her, too. She was his best friend.

The approach Kevin would have used to end the relationship not only would have been very offensive to Lee, but probably would have failed. I've witnessed these "final" good-byes and there's nothing final about them. All they do is leave the wayward spouse and the lover even more convinced that they belong with each other.

From Lee's perspective (and mine), Amy was the worst enemy of Kevin and Lee's marriage. She stood in the way of their happiness and the happiness of their children. Lee did not want Kevin to "let Amy down gently."

I recommended to Kevin that he write Amy the final good-bye in a letter. I did not want him to see or talk to her ever again if at all possible.

The letter had to be written in a way that was acceptable to Lee. It was to be short and to the point. It was to begin with a statement of how selfish it was to cause those they love so much pain, and while marital reconciliation cannot completely repay the offense, it would be the right thing to do. Then Kevin would explain how he cared about Lee and his children, and for the sake of their protection had decided to completely end his relationship with Amy. Kevin would promise never to see or communicate with Amy again in life and would ask Amy to respect that promise. Nothing would be said about how he would miss her.

At first Kevin felt that such a letter would be a cruel way to end his affair. But he eventually understood how important it was to completely close the door on any hope of a future relationship. It was over, and Amy needed to know that. If Kevin had given Amy any false hope, preventing her from moving on in her life, that would have been incredibly cruel.

Kevin wrote this letter to Amy and let Lee read it:

Amy, I want you to know that out of respect and love for my wife and children, I have come to realize that I must never see or talk with you again. My relationship with you was a cruel indul-

gence that Lee did not deserve. While I cannot completely repay Lee for the pain I have caused her, I will do my best to become the husband she has been missing. I care a great deal for my family and I would not want to do anything to risk their happiness. I will not make any further contact with you and I do not want you to make any contact with me. Please respect my desire to end our relationship.

Sincerely, Kevin.

A mutual friend was asked to deliver the letter to Amy so that there would be no opportunity for Kevin to add anything to its content. I told Kevin that he should not call Amy. It's very tempting for a wayward spouse to tell the lover that the letter is not entirely his or hers, but rather one that the spouse and counselor wrote.

Extraordinary Precautions Must Be Taken to Guarantee Separation

An affair is not only extremely destructive to a marriage, but it is also extremely difficult to end. So Kevin's willingness to end his relationship with Amy had to be reinforced with extraordinary precautions that would make it difficult for them to contact each other again.

1. Changing Jobs and Relocating

As long as Amy and Kevin worked together, the goal of total separation was impossible to achieve. So Kevin had to take the extraordinary precaution of trying to find another job where he would not be working with Amy. Kevin's management job would be difficult to give up, especially since Lee was a stay-at-home mom. She had been out of the workplace for quite a few years and would not be able to earn much even if she were to get a job right away.

I suggested to Kevin that he speak with his boss at work and explain his situation. As it turns out, the auto dealership was one of several owned by the same man, so Kevin was able to move laterally to a similar position at another dealership. But many of the people I counsel do not have such an easy time making a job change. They must take vacation time to look for other work and sometimes remain unemployed for months before a suitable new job becomes available.

Most wayward spouses don't think they need to quit a job or move to a new location. They feel they have themselves under control, and this extraordinary precaution is unnecessary. Sometimes they insist on a trial period where their commitment can be tested. But a trial period is just an opportunity for the affair to reignite.

Changing jobs or moving to a new location is usually a difficult and costly choice. Yet, it can be done, and without this extraordinary measure, the risk of an affair spinning out of control is very great. Easy access to a former lover must be avoided at all costs.

> *Easy access to a former lover must be avoided at all costs.*

Of course, if Amy had decided to quit her job voluntarily, then Kevin would not have had to change jobs. I've seen many cases in which, after an affair is exposed, the lover is the one who moves away, and then it is not necessary for the spouse to change jobs or relocate.

Sometimes a couple will decide to relocate, even if the lover has left the area. After the agony of an affair, it's often very helpful to move to new surroundings and start over. Otherwise, everything they see and do keeps reminding them of the affair.

2. Blocking Communication with a Lover

Even when a family has moved from one coast to the other, the telephone is readily available to make contact with a former lover. After the sacrifice of a job change or physical relocation, wayward spouses have been known to keep an affair alive through the phone, e-mail, pagers, and voice mail.

One man I counseled had ended his affair and was two months into marital recovery when his ex-lover sent him an e-mail. That was all it took to reignite the flame of their relationship, making it more intense and discreet than ever.

Since these forms of communication are a tempting way to make contact with an ex-lover, measures should be taken to make them difficult to use for that purpose. I suggest that a couple use an unlisted home number, change their e-mail address and pager number, and have the betrayed spouse monitor all voice messages and mail. Most important, I suggest that the betrayed spouse have free access to records of telephone calls and e-mail. These precautions may make a wayward spouse feel like a convict on probation, but they are often essential conditions to breaking the addiction that keeps an affair alive.

At first Kevin didn't think such extraordinary precautions were needed. He felt strongly that Amy would not try to contact him once he broke it off with her. But he had his phone number changed anyway. Lee listened to all recorded telephone messages and opened his mail to make sure he did not receive any messages from Amy. One day Lee discovered a letter from Amy. In it she told Kevin how much she missed him. Lee told Kevin about Amy's letter but did not describe the contents. They both agreed that Lee should destroy the letter, which is what she did. That experience helped Kevin see how important it was for him to follow my extraordinary precautions.

3. Accounting for Time

In every marriage, decisions about time should be made together by the husband and wife. They should work out their schedules with mutual agreement, because the way each of them spends his or her time affects the other. Mutual agreement regarding how time is spent guarantees a thoughtful schedule. Besides, both spouses need to know where the other one is in case of emergencies.

Because an affair depends on the health of a secret second life, a wayward spouse must be able to spend at least some of his or her time away from the watchful eye of the betrayed spouse. So it's important to do whatever it takes to assure that time is accounted for throughout the day and night. That's especially true when an affair is first discovered and the wayward spouse is willing to end it.

I suggested to Kevin and Lee that they give each other a twenty-four-hour schedule of their daily activities. With the schedule, there would be a telephone number where they could be reached. I explained that it was something they should have been doing throughout their marriage out of consideration for each other. Knowing where Kevin was twenty-four hours a day and being able to contact him also helped Lee restore her trust in Kevin.

I suggested that they call each other several times during the day, just to talk, but also for Lee to be assured that Kevin was where he said he would be.

Kevin and Lee began giving each other daily schedules. Kevin actually looked forward to Lee's calls. He also was pleasantly surprised when she stopped by his office. He enjoyed getting the attention he had missed during most of their marriage.

Kevin called Lee when he left the office each day, so she would know when he would be home. It was something he should have done throughout his marriage, but he just never got into the habit. What started as a way for Lee to check up on Kevin soon became a way for them to show their care and concern for each other.

4. Accounting for Money

Just as decisions about the use of time should be made together by a husband and wife, so should financial decisions be made jointly. This is the only way to be sure that the interests of both spouses are considered. So when I suggested to Kevin that Lee should be aware of and approve all the money he spends, I was not just imposing yet another cruel hardship as punishment for his error. But he took it that way.

> *A secret second life depends not only on hidden time, but also on hidden money.*

A secret second life depends not only on hidden time, but also on hidden money. Lee usually didn't know how Kevin spent their money, and so it would have been easy for him to divert some of his income to a secret second life.

As Kevin and Amy were developing their relationship, he took her to lunch and bought her token gifts. He wasn't spending a lot of money, but he wouldn't have been able to hide the expense from Lee if she were involved on a daily basis in managing their finances.

Kevin had given Lee very little financial information. He earned the money and paid the bills. He gave her an allowance for groceries and incidental expenses, and the rest was his to do with as he pleased.

You can see why my suggestion that he make all financial decisions jointly with Lee seemed like punishment.

Granted, accounting for how he spent his money was partially intended to be a precaution to help Kevin avoid contact with Amy, but even more important, accounting for money was essential in helping Kevin and Lee build a strong and caring marriage. It wasn't punishment at all—it was the foundation of a thoughtful relationship, in which the money they spent would be mutually beneficial. Eventually Kevin also saw it that way.

5. Spending Leisure Time Together

Kevin and Amy had become each other's best friends partly because they spent much of their leisure time with each other. They not only exercised together every morning, but they also had lunch with each other and often spent time together after work.

We have already discussed the importance of accounting for time, especially leisure time. But another extraordinary precaution that a wayward spouse and betrayed spouse should take is to spend their leisure time together.

So I encouraged Lee and Kevin to be together whenever he was not at work. Lee now realized that it was vital to their relationship that she spend more time with Kevin. By using day care and a friend with whom she exchanged baby-sitting duties, Lee was often able to join Kevin for lunch. They also joined a new health club and exercised together three mornings a week.

Once in a while Kevin was required to take a business trip. Since I encouraged them to spend all their leisure time together, Lee went along with him. They were curious to know how long this extraordinary precaution would be necessary, since it was expensive and inconvenient for Lee to travel with Kevin every time he was gone overnight. My response was that the risk of an affair was too great to take any chances. Besides, after they had traveled together for a while, they would probably want to do it the rest of their lives.

When There's Less Emotional Attachment

The deep emotional attachment of soul-mate affairs make them very difficult to end. That's why I recommend the five extraordinary precautions. When these measures are taken, success can usually be guaranteed.

But what about affairs with less emotional attachment? And what about one-night stands? Is it really necessary to totally separate a wayward spouse from a lover in these situations?

I recommend the five extraordinary precautions for all types of affairs, even one-night stands, for two reasons. First, any contact a wayward spouse has with a former lover is an offense to a betrayed spouse. Once a sexual relationship has occurred, or even threatens to occur, further contact should be eliminated out of consideration to the spouse.

My second reason is that it's difficult to judge the degree of attachment between the lovers in affairs, so precautions must be taken just in case the attachment is greater than the wayward spouse admits. A wayward spouse in love will often argue that he or she has no emotional feelings toward the lover, as a ploy to try to continue the relationship. If there really is no attachment, then the extraordinary precautions I recommend will simply be easier to implement.

When a wayward spouse has a history of one-night stands, I usually suggest that they find a career that does not require their being away from home overnight, or one that allows the betrayed spouse to travel with the wayward spouse. This worked for Lee and Kevin. She joined him on his infrequent business trips. But what if he had been an interstate truck driver, away from home a week at a time? Would Lee have had to travel with him cross-country?

It's been done! Some betrayed spouses I've counseled have made the decision to drive with their spouse over the road to avoid affairs. In fact one enjoyed the experience so much, that when her husband died unexpectedly, she tried to marry another trucker so that she could continue the lifestyle she had come to enjoy. But in cases where a betrayed spouse is not willing or able to travel, the wayward spouse should change careers so that they can be together every night.

I believe that the extraordinary precautions I recommend do more than help couples end marriage-threatening affairs—they also help a couple form the kind of relationship they always wanted. And that's the best reason to use my extraordinary precautions for separating a wayward spouse from a lover—they not only help separate them, but they also help create a strong marriage. These conditions are not a punishment for unfaithfulness; they are crucial building blocks that form the foundation for a strong marital recovery.

> The extraordinary precautions do more than end marriage-threatening affairs; they help a couple form the kind of relationship they always wanted.

These recommendations may seem rigid, unnecessarily confining, and even paranoid to those who have not been the victim of infidelity. But people like Sue and Jon, who have suffered unimaginable pain as a result of an affair that spun out of control, can easily see their value. For the inconvenience of following my advice, Sue would have spared herself and Jon the very worst experience of their lives.

Checklist for How to End an Affair the Right Way: Total Separation from the Lover

_____ Wayward spouse should reveal information about the affair to the betrayed spouse.

_____ Wayward spouse should make a commitment to the betrayed spouse to never see or talk to the lover again.

_____ Wayward spouse should write a letter to the lover ending the relationship and send it with the approval of the betrayed spouse.

_____ Wayward spouse should take extraordinary precautions to guarantee total separation from the lover:

    _____ Change jobs and relocate if necessary.

    _____ Block potential communication with the lover (change e-mail address and telephone, cell phone, and pager numbers; have voice messages and mail monitored by the betrayed spouse).

    _____ Account for time (betrayed spouse and wayward spouse give each other a twenty-four-hour daily schedule with locations and telephone numbers).

    _____ Account for money (betrayed spouse and wayward spouse give each other a complete account of all money spent, and they make all financial decisions jointly).

    _____ Spend leisure time together.

Preparing for Marital Recovery

When Kevin decided to end his relationship with Amy, he made the right decision. But he didn't make that decision just once. In the days that followed he had to make the decision many times. He was tempted to give Amy a call every day just to hear her voice and every day he made the decision not to call her.

How long will this last? Kevin wanted to know. *I'm not sure I can do this much longer.* Only three days had passed since he had talked to Amy last, and he was already overwhelmed by the pain of being separated from her. He was just a phone call away from ending that pain—by just talking to her.

I did my best to encourage Kevin. Antidepressant medication prescribed by his doctor also helped relieve some of his most intense feelings of hopelessness. But it was Kevin's willingness to follow the five extraordinary precautions that actually kept him away from Amy (see pages 59–63).

Getting through Withdrawal

Kevin was going through an experience that those familiar with addiction know all too well—withdrawal—the emotional reaction a person experiences when separated from the object of his or her addiction. Before his marital recovery could begin, he had to get through this temporary, but painful, experience.

> *Marital recovery cannot begin until withdrawal has ended.*

The feelings of withdrawal and grief are very similar. They are both emotional reactions that are associated with the loss of a very valuable part of one's life, something that provided great pleasure and satisfaction. In the case of grief, the loss is usually final—loss of a home by fire or a loved one by death. However, in the case of withdrawal, whether from alcohol or a lover, the loss doesn't have to be final. All that's needed to recover the loss is to return to the object of addiction. And that's why Kevin was faced with hundreds of decisions to leave Amy—he could have her back any time he wanted.

During the first few weeks after total separation from a lover, the depression that accompanies the loss can be so pervasive and overwhelming that nothing makes the wayward spouse happy. That was certainly Kevin's experience. There was no escape from the loss that he felt. He simply had to get through the withdrawal period before he could enjoy his life again.

Lee wanted to quickly straighten out whatever had been missing in her marriage. That's what most spouses do when they get over the shock of discovering that their spouse was unfaithful. If it was sex that was missing, the spouse wants to offer more and better sex. If it was affection, it's more and better affection. If it was conversation, more and better conversation. A spouse is usually willing to do whatever it takes to regain a wayward spouse's love. But these initial efforts to meet the wayward spouse's emotional needs are usually ineffective during the first few weeks of withdrawal because the spouse is so unhappy.

I warned Lee that there would not be much she could do to cheer up Kevin. Her love and care for him during the first few weeks of his separation from Amy would probably seem to her as wasted effort. However, after the worst symptoms of withdrawal began to fade, those extraordinary precautions I had recommended would help Lee and Kevin redeposit love units into each other's Love Bank.

An Affair Offers No Painless Escape

Kevin may have suffered after he separated from Amy. But by separating early in the affair, he spared himself, Lee, and his children untold additional suffering that they would have experienced if he had not separated from her when he did.

But Sue and Jon were not spared that additional suffering. Although Sue tried to separate from Greg after Jon discovered their affair, her failure to take extraordinary precautions to guarantee separation caused her and her family so much pain that it almost ruined their lives. Most people who have affairs are like Sue—they don't do what it takes to make a clean break with their lover. Sue lost perspective for what was important in her life. She was willing to sacrifice her children, her reputation, and her financial security just to continue her relationship with Greg. The inability to separate makes the tragedy of an affair much more painful than it would be if the lovers separated early on.

When people like Sue try to leave their lover and experience the pain of withdrawal, they often cannot resist the temptation to return to the affair. But returning to the lover does not alleviate their depression for long. In fact for many, the momentary emotional relief after reconciliation with the lover is followed by depression returning with a vengeance. After returning to the lover, it doesn't usually take long before the wayward spouse feels so depressed they consider suicide as their only escape. They cannot imagine leaving their lover, nor can they imagine leaving their family. They see no hope. They know they are causing their spouse and children unbearable pain, yet they seem powerless to stop the affair.

Sue told me, *I know what I am doing is stupid. I'm going to lose everything but I just can't leave my lover. I'd rather hit bottom than have to choose between Greg and my family.* Sadly her statement was very prophetic—she did hit bottom. She almost lost everything to stay with Greg just a little longer.

The pain of total separation from a lover is great at first but it eventually comes to an end, and marital recovery can then begin. The alternative—not separating—keeps suffering alive as long as the affair continues. Clearly, the choice to end the affair once and for all is the least painful of the two alternatives.

Kevin anticipated that it would be difficult to leave Amy but he had no idea how powerful his emotional reactions would be. Within a day of his decision, he began experiencing a depression that he had never felt before. He couldn't eat or sleep. All he could think about was Amy.

> The pain of total separation from a lover is great at first but it eventually comes to an end, and marital recovery can then begin.

The Symptoms of Withdrawal

Someone going through withdrawal usually experiences depression, anxiety, and anger—all in a very intense form. The feeling of utter hopelessness, the fear of making a catastrophic mistake, and even anger toward a betrayed spouse are overwhelming. These reactions are usually so severe that I often suggest that the wayward spouse consult with his or her doctor for antidepressant medication to help stabilize these symptoms during this most unpleasant experience.

But if there is total separation from the lover, the most intense symptoms of withdrawal usually last only about three weeks and then fade over the next six months. As I mentioned earlier, if a slip occurs and contact is made with a lover during withdrawal, the clock goes back to zero, and the period of withdrawal starts all over again. So those few who report lingering withdrawal symptoms after six months are usually guilty of making sporadic contacts with the former lover, and lying about those contacts to their spouse.

Lee was concerned about Kevin's depression. She had never seen him react this way before. I had warned both of them that the symptoms of withdrawal were almost inevitable, but the warning did not prepare her for the extreme form they took. At first, Kevin experienced a total loss of energy and could hardly face each day. In reality, events were turning out to his advantage, but through the fog of his depression, he couldn't see anything but doom and gloom. For example, even though his boss was very understanding and cooperative, offering him a job at another dealership, Kevin came away feeling as though the meeting had been a disaster.

Kevin was spending all of his nonworking hours with Lee and his children—these were my instructions—but Kevin's depression rubbed off on Lee and made her feel depressed too. After a few days, neither of them were sure it was a good idea to be together.

They were in a necessary, but very temporary, holding pattern, during which their relationship wasn't going anywhere. Kevin's symptoms of withdrawal had to fade significantly before his marital recovery could begin. But being together was still an important step in preparing for the recovery process. They had to be together to prevent Kevin's return to Amy.

It was important that they avoid anger, disrespect, or demands while they were together. They were to simply keep each other company for a few weeks and avoid doing anything that would make matters worse. Opportunities to meet each other's emotional needs would come later.

The exercise that Lee was getting three mornings a week with Kevin helped keep her emotionally stable. The assurances I gave her also helped keep her in a positive mood. But if she had become as depressed as Kevin, I would have encouraged her to consult with her doctor for the same antidepressant medication Kevin was using. The time it takes for withdrawal to end seems like an eternity when it is taking place, but the worst is usually over in about a month. I kept reminding Lee of that fact.

Kevin and Lee followed my suggestions to ensure separation from Amy. Kevin gave Lee a schedule of his daily activities, and she gave him hers. They exercised together and called each other during the day, and Kevin spent as much time as possible with Lee.

Some of the best examples of recovery I've witnessed involved couples who were forced, due to a prior business or vacation commitment, to be together almost twenty-four hours a day for about a month during withdrawal. It's the perfect formula for withdrawal because it ensures total separation from a lover.

Most couples, however, are not fortunate enough to have such advantageous preplanning. So I often recommend an extended vacation or successive weekend getaways for a couple going through withdrawal. The wayward spouse's depression is often so severe that getting away from everything can provide a welcome relief.

Granted, for the betrayed spouse, taking a vacation after such trauma may, at first, seem like "sleeping with the enemy." But it provides a great opportunity to be together in a comfortable setting that minimizes the withdrawal of love units and maximizes their deposit.

The extraordinary precautions worked for Kevin and Lee. Kevin did not talk to Amy again, and the intense emotional reaction, which he experienced initially, faded within a few weeks.

What about Withdrawal after a One-Night Stand?

A spouse who engages in one-night stands is not usually addicted to a particular lover—the addiction is to one-night stands. For that reason the extraordinary precautions I recommend to separate a spouse from a lover also work well to separate a spouse from one-night stands or any other form of sex to which he or she may be addicted. And that separation creates the same symptoms of withdrawal that Kevin experienced. But it's not possible to begin marital recovery until one-night stands, or any other type of extramarital sexual behavior, are ended once and for all, and the feeling of withdrawal that follows their elimination fades away.

Regardless of the type of affair or sexual addiction—one-night stands, relationships with soul mates, or anything in-between—separation from the object of addiction and recovery from the symptoms of withdrawal must take place before marital reconciliation is possible.

What If the Wayward Spouse Contacts the Lover?

As you will see in my plan for recovery, honesty is crucial in creating a good marriage. And it's also crucial for totally separating from a lover. A question that I encouraged Lee to ask Kevin was, *Have you seen or talked to Amy today?* Kevin promised that he would answer that question honestly whenever Lee asked. He even tried to remember to tell her whether or not he had seen or talked to Amy, before Lee asked him.

I prepared Lee for the possibility that Kevin might admit that he had contacted Amy. Her reaction to that honest revelation would be very important. She was to take a deep breath and say, *Thank you for being honest with me.* Then they were to discuss what they could do in the future to avoid such contact again.

If there is a failure to totally separate from a lover, it usually means that the measures taken to guarantee separation are inadequate. Perhaps Kevin's job at another dealership would not enable him to separate entirely from Amy. She may have come uninvited to the dealership to talk to him. In that case, a relocation to another city or state would be the answer.

> If there is a failure to totally separate from a lover, it usually means that the measures taken to guarantee separation are inadequate.

An alternative to relocation would be for Kevin to take a three-month leave of absence from his job, preventing Amy from walking in on him at will. During those three months, Amy's symptoms of withdrawal would probably subside enough for her to honor his request for her never to talk to him again.

Any contact with Amy, initiated by either Kevin or Amy, would set Kevin's period of withdrawal back to the beginning. The feeling of depression that would have started to fade would be more intense after seeing her again. But it would not mean an end to the plan for marital recovery. It would just set the recovery back to the beginning. Hopefully, Kevin would agree to new conditions that would make contact with Amy less likely.

What If the Wayward Spouse Doesn't Want to Totally Separate from the Lover?

After a series of failures to separate, it may become apparent that any reasonable conditions to separate cannot prevent a wayward spouse to persist in contacting the lover. Or the wayward spouse may refuse to follow the conditions to separate.

Sue had made a genuine effort to meet the conditions that would help her avoid seeing Greg—for about a week. But then she broke down and contacted him and secretly reestablished her relationship with him. As part of her deception, she tried to make Jon think she was following my conditions for separation.

But it soon became apparent to Sue that she couldn't really follow my conditions and still see Greg as often as she wanted. At first, she gave plausible excuses for her failure to meet the conditions of separation. But when those excuses finally didn't work, she became increasingly dishonest and defensive. Her lies were eventually revealed and Sue left Jon to avoid the conditions that had separated her from Greg. Away from Jon and on her own, she was free to be with Greg without any interference or explanation.

Jon was tempted to divorce Sue at each new phase of their nightmare. Was there a point at which Jon should have divorced Sue and simply ended it all? Should he have divorced her when he first found her in bed with Greg? Should he have divorced her when she refused to follow the measures to guarantee total separation? Or when she left to live in her own apartment? Or when she had Jon move out of his own house so she could return? Or should he have divorced her when Greg finally left her, and she had burned all of her bridges?

> While there is no hope for reconciliation when the affair is underway, as soon as the affair is ended, reconciliation is definitely possible.

Many people don't agree with my efforts to save such a marriage. They feel that once a spouse is unfaithful, the marriage should end. But I was able to convince Jon to wait. *Wait for what?* Jon would ask in deep frustration. *Wait until you have a chance to regain her love for you,* was my answer. *Wait until the affair has ended and she is willing to try to reconcile with you.*

Many would lack the patience to wait as long as Jon waited, but I knew that he had history on his side. Affairs usually end and when they do, the wayward spouse is usually willing to rebuild the marriage.

Most affairs do not end like Kevin's affair, with a willingness to totally separate from the lover. Most affairs, like Sue's, continue on after they are first discovered.

You may think that after a spouse willfully chooses a lover and abandons the family, there would be no hope for marital reconciliation, but that's not true. While there is no hope for reconciliation when the affair is underway, as soon as the affair is ended, reconciliation is definitely possible. And almost all affairs end sooner than most people think they will.

But for the betrayed spouse, waiting for the affair to end seems like an eternity. The wayward spouse can't seem to make up his or her mind—one moment committing to the marriage and the next moment committing to the lover. To help a betrayed spouse survive that painful period of vacillation—the time it takes for an affair to die a natural death—I recommend two plans. If the first plan (plan A) is unsuccessful in separating the wayward spouse from the lover, the second plan (plan B) is followed until the affair is ended. This sequence—plan A followed by plan B—represents the most sensible approach to handling a wayward spouse's inability to decide between the lover and the betrayed spouse.

Plan A: Avoid Angry Outbursts, Disrespect, and Demands at All Costs

Jon made a good point when he asked, *Why should I care about Sue's feelings? She doesn't care about mine.* She had cheated and lied to him over and over again. Why should he treat her any differently than she had treated him? Jon was very angry and felt that what Sue needed was a healthy dose of reality. He was tempted to give her a piece of his mind.

How could I expect Jon to avoid burning his bridges after Sue had behaved so thoughtlessly? I offered him four reasons to try a plan that would give his marriage a chance to recover.

1. **Jon was partly responsible for Sue's affair.** Jon knew, deep down inside, that his career choices had a great deal to do with Sue's affair. His work schedule prevented him from meeting her emotional needs, and it made her vulnerable to Greg's attention. Even after she was willing to reconcile with him, his job continued to take priority. He now realized what he should have done to help prevent her affair and he needed a chance to prove it to her. He would have that chance if he could be patient.

2. **Sue had not yet decided to end her marriage.** She was trying to justify her affair in terms of Jon's failure to care about her feelings. Whenever he was angry, disrespectful, or demand-

ing, it tended to support Sue's belief that she had chosen the wrong man to marry, a man who was a tyrant at heart. But there was also a part of her that wanted to believe that Jon was the right man for her. I wanted Jon to support the part of Sue that felt she had married the right man, and prove wrong the part of her that thought he was a tyrant.

3. **Jon needed to know that he had done his best to save their marriage.** If Jon were to take the initiative to divorce Sue, he would be burdened by guilt, particularly after he saw the effect of the divorce on his children. He would always wonder if he had done all he could do to save the marriage. If, instead of seeking a divorce, he showed his care for Sue under these horrible conditions of infidelity, it would be a good example to his children of how to care for others, even when others don't always show their care in return. Then, if the marriage were to end in divorce, he would have fewer regrets.

4. **If Jon followed my plan, and it failed, he would no longer have any feelings of love for Sue.** In spite of Sue's affair, Jon was still in love with her. If their marriage had ended in divorce before he followed my plan, he would have missed her terribly. But my plan offered him something that would make a divorce much less painful—he would lose his love for her. The plan had the effect of withdrawing so many love units from Sue's account in his Love Bank that if their marriage ended in divorce, his love for her would be completely gone.

Plan A was simple to understand but difficult to implement. Jon was to avoid doing anything that would upset Sue. Anger, disrespect, and demands were to be completely eliminated. The only thing he could do that might upset her was ask her questions about her compliance with the conditions of separation she had agreed to follow.

What made plan A particularly hard for Jon to implement was Sue's blatant disregard for his feelings. How could he avoid upsetting Sue when just about everything *she* was doing upset *him?* For that reason, I suggested a time limit for plan A. Quite frankly, there's a limit to everyone's patience, and Jon was no exception.

Jon agreed to a six-month time limit, which is about average for most of the couples I counsel in his position. During those six months, he would try to avoid doing anything that would upset Sue.

At the same time, if she would let him, he would try to meet her emotional needs.

I warned Jon that as long as Sue was involved with Greg, she would give Jon little opportunity to meet her needs. The time and attention she had always wanted from Jon were now received from Greg. But I still wanted him to offer to meet her needs anyway, just in case she decided to give him another chance.

Sue was still living with Jon at home, and once in a while, it seemed that Jon was making real progress. Sue would warm up to him and would even tell him that she loved him. He had learned his lesson about business trips and had obtained a job transfer that did not require him to travel. His new job allowed him the time to meet Sue's emotional needs, if she'd let him. But from time to time there would be a setback, and she would return to a more defensive posture.

As long as Sue continued to see Greg, she vacillated back and forth between Jon and Greg, and that drove Jon nuts. But he did everything he could to avoid withdrawing love units. For almost six months, Jon made every effort to avoid angry outbursts, disrespectful judgments, and demands, even when he knew Sue was lying to him and sneaking out to be with Greg. Jon did not tell Sue about his time limit, because she would have interpreted it as a threat—a demand for her to leave Greg. However, he did remind her repeatedly that he loved her and wanted the opportunity to meet her needs.

Sue didn't make it easy for Jon to express his feelings for her. In fact whenever they were together, she either left the room or avoided looking at him when he tried to tell her he still loved her. How was Jon supposed to communicate with her when she didn't want to talk to him? I offered him two suggestions: letters and telephone.

I've found that wayward spouses have an easier time handling their emotional reactions when they do not have to look at the betrayed spouse. Besides, letters and telephone calls are much safer from both spouses' perspective. Jon was able to choose his words carefully whenever he wrote Sue a letter, and when he called her from work on the phone, either of them could end the conversation at will. That made those conversations much more comfortable.

I tried to help Jon write letters that expressed to Sue what he had learned and what he would like to do to resolve their problems. These letters allowed Jon to think through his own thoughts so that he would accurately convey his feelings without expressing anger, disrespect, or demands.

Jon did an outstanding job of not saying or doing anything that would make Sue feel uncomfortable living with him. But it was the affair itself that made her uncomfortable. Whenever Jon asked about her activities, she lied to him, and that made her feel guilty about her lies and about what she was lying about. She had always considered herself to be an honest person, but now her lies proved otherwise. And whenever she thought about the person she had become, it made her feel very depressed and guilty.

> *Affairs and dishonesty always go hand in hand. You cannot have one without the other.*

Affairs and dishonesty always go hand in hand. You cannot have one without the other. The only way for Sue to become honest again was for her to separate totally from Greg. But without separation, she could not be honest, and without honesty, she could not be comfortable living with Jon.

Our six-month time limit for plan A was never completed. Before the time had expired, Sue made the decision to leave Jon and move into her own apartment. For many, that would have been the last straw, but for Jon it was actually part of the plan, moved up a little in time. He was now ready for plan B.

For many couples, plan A gets the job done. The thoughtfulness demonstrated by the betrayed spouse helps a wayward spouse make the decision to permanently separate from the lover. But even when plan A doesn't stop an affair, having used it makes marital reconciliation much easier if separation from the lover ever does occur. The care shown in plan A helps make the betrayed spouse an attractive choice for the wayward spouse when the affair dies a natural death. It also proves that the betrayed spouse knows how to protect the wayward spouse from anger, disrespect, and demands, even under conditions of infidelity. It offers hope that he or she can be trusted to continue to protect the wayward spouse after the affair is over. And the betrayed spouse's willingness to meet the emotional needs that the lover was meeting also offers hope for reconciliation.

Another advantage to plan A is that when it ends, the betrayed spouse leaves the wayward spouse with the best possible memories of how he or she was treated. When Sue separated from Jon, she left with the memory that he had been considerate of her feelings and he had tried to meet her emotional needs.

Plan B: Avoid Contact with the Wayward Spouse until the Affair Has Ended

In most affairs, the betrayed spouse meets some of the wayward spouse's emotional needs, and the lover meets other needs. When Sue and Jon were living together, and she was having the affair with Greg, she had the best of both worlds. With Greg she had conversation, affection, and companionship and with Jon she had financial support and family commitment. It was an uncomfortable juggling act for Sue, but her needs were being met. If Jon had not asked so many questions and made it so difficult for Sue to sneak off to be with Greg, she would have let this go on indefinitely. But this would have been unfair and emotionally exhausting for Jon.

This is where plan B comes in. If the wayward spouse will not totally separate from the lover, then plan B separates the betrayed spouse—and the needs he or she met—from the wayward spouse. It is a taste of what is to come if divorce actually takes place.

But doesn't plan B throw the wayward spouse into the waiting arms of the lover? Doesn't it give the affair the chance it needs to succeed?

> *Most affairs are based on fantasy and wishful thinking.*

Most affairs are based on fantasy and wishful thinking. In reality, the lover is not an improvement over the betrayed spouse, and giving an affair a chance can actually prove that the relationship won't succeed. Love units were deposited into Greg's account in Sue's Love Bank because they were *not* together as husband and wife, battling through the tough problems of daily living. They were together only when Sue was escaping the hard realities of her life. By taking Jon out of Sue's life, and letting Greg become involved in all aspects of her life, Greg's ability to handle her problems was put to the test. And, like most lovers when tested, Greg failed.

By the time Sue moved out, Jon had almost come to the end of his rope. If he had stayed with Sue much longer, he would probably not have been able to control his emotional reactions and would have risked becoming very disrespectful.

If Sue had not left Jon first, he would have moved away from home. I usually suggest moving to a place where a betrayed spouse can be surrounded by those who love and care for him or her. A strong support group is needed during a time of separation. And a betrayed spouse needs to be far away from the wayward spouse and his or her lover. I often go so far as to recommend moving to another city or state. But people who have custody of children are often not able to do this because they cannot legally move the children out of the state. I suggest consulting with an attorney to learn how state laws may limit such a move.

Sue's first week away from home was so hard on her emotionally that she actually returned before Jon had a chance to implement plan B. And some of their discussions were so hopeful that Jon felt plan B would not be necessary. But I warned him to expect the worst, and sadly that's what happened.

After a week Sue moved back to her apartment, and it was clear that she would be there for some time. It was then that Jon implemented plan B. He made arrangements with their mutual friends Jane and Paul to handle all necessary communication so that he would not need to see or talk to Sue unless they happened to accidentally cross paths.

Sue did not understand the full implications of leaving Jon. She thought it would give her more freedom to be with Greg but she didn't know about plan B.

I helped Jon write a letter to Sue explaining what he planned to do during their separation and what she would be required to do to reconcile.

My Dear Sue,

I apologize to you for my part in creating an environment that helped make your affair with Greg possible. I foolishly pursued my career without understanding my responsibility to meet your most important emotional needs. I was not there for you when you needed me the most, and we are now both suffering for my mistake.

I am willing to avoid the mistakes I've made in the past and create a new life for both of us that will meet your needs. But I can–

not do that until you end your relationship with Greg once and for all.

Until then, I will avoid seeing you or talking to you. I will also not be able to help you financially. Our friends Jane and Paul have agreed to help make arrangements for you to visit the children whenever you would like. But I will not be here when you visit. If you want to communicate about the children or any other matter, it will have to be through Jane and Paul.

I ask you to respect my decision to separate from you this way. You must know about the suffering I have endured because of your relationship with Greg, and I simply cannot be with you any longer, knowing that you are with him. I still love you but I cannot see you under these conditions.

As soon as you are willing to permanently separate from Greg and are willing to follow the measures that were suggested to ensure total separation, I will be willing to discuss our future together.

I want us to be able to rebuild our marriage some day. I want us to be able to meet each other's emotional needs and to avoid doing anything to hurt each other. We need to build a new lifestyle in which everything we do makes us both happy. Then there will never again be a reason for us to separate. I want to be your best friend, someone who is always there for you when you need me. And I want you as my best friend.

I loved you when we married and I continue to love you right up to this day. I just cannot be with you or help you as long as you are seeing Greg.

With my love,
Jon

Jon delivered the letter to Sue and he also sent a copy to Greg with a note at the bottom saying:

I love Sue with all my heart and am willing to do whatever it takes to make her happy. I will wait for her to give me that chance.

Sue did not miss talking to Jon, she did not miss his affection, nor did she miss his companionship, because those needs were being met by Greg. But she sure missed his money. At first, she wanted to be completely on her own and she had saved to prepare for her independence. But those savings ran out much faster than she realized, and the money she earned was not nearly enough to pay for the lifestyle she had come to enjoy.

Plan B was designed to help Sue discover that all of her needs could not be met by Greg. To achieve that objective, Jon had to stop meeting those needs for a while and let Greg try to meet them. But plan B was crippled by Sue's counselor, who advised her to return home and kick Jon out. Her attorney also advised her to get a legal separation and a court order for Jon to pay her three thousand dollars a month in child support shortly after she returned home. He was forced by law to meet part of her need for financial support.

Still, plan B was helpful to Jon. His separation from Sue protected him from experiencing much of the pain he had tried to endure when they were living together. Money was not the only thing that Jon had provided Sue—he had also provided care and security for her children. While he was at home with his daughters, the girls had hoped that their mother would eventually return to them and that their family would be reunited. But when Sue did return, she forced Jon to leave his girls, something they had not anticipated. They were both very resentful toward Sue for forcing him to leave. They missed their dad terribly and blamed Sue for creating the situation.

Sue now had money and the comfort of her home, but her children, whom she loved dearly, were devastated. They had liked Greg and his boys, but now they resented Greg because their mom was trying to replace their dad with him. It was not a happy homecoming for Sue.

Jon's family and friends were all advising him to divorce Sue. They had a very difficult time understanding what he could possibly hope to achieve by enduring the pain and humiliation that she was inflicting on him. But Jon was determined to try my plan B. And just as plan A had a deadline, Jon and I decided on a deadline for plan B.

Most affairs last less than six months after they are exposed to the light of day. A very few may survive two years of sunlight but that is rare, especially when a betrayed spouse lets go and gives the affair a chance to destroy itself. Jon had already agreed to a six-month deadline for plan A, so he added another eighteen months for plan B—a total of two years. If that time had expired without reconciliation, he would have divorced Sue.

But Sue's affair ended just as most affairs end. In some cases, it's the wayward spouse that realizes that the lover cannot offer enough to compensate for the loss of his or her marriage. In other cases, like Sue's, it's the lover that realizes that the wayward spouse is not worth the hassle. When Greg was seeing Sue in secret, their relationship was filled with excitement and anticipation. But when it was out into the open, the problems of real life, and their inability to solve them, torpedoed the fun they had together.

> *Most affairs last less than six months after they are exposed to the light of day.*

Sue was depressed most of the time, and there was nothing Greg could do to lift her spirits. Her girls became outwardly hostile toward him, and he found his relationship with Sue increasingly difficult. No love units were being deposited into her account in his Love Bank and many were being withdrawn. Eventually there were none left. So he began a relationship with another woman who did not have children and ended his relationship with Sue. If he had not ended it, I'm sure that Sue would have eventually ended it herself.

Even so, Sue was devastated when Greg left her. She had given up almost everything to have Greg with her, and now he was gone. She was left with her house, her children, and Jon's financial support. But now there was no one to meet her other emotional needs—no one, that is, but Jon.

Is an Apology Necessary?

Sue told her friends Jane and Paul that she was finally willing to totally separate from Greg and she wanted to give her marriage with Jon a chance to recover. So they relayed the message to Jon. Sue and Jon then met together for dinner to discuss reconciliation.

After all that Sue had put Jon through, you'd think she would have returned to him humbled and deeply remorseful. Sometimes a wayward spouse does ask for forgiveness for the incredible thoughtlessness of his or her affair, but Sue didn't. In fact the way she talked to Jon about getting back together sounded as if he was the one who had had the affair. She made it seem as if he was lucky to have another chance to win her back.

A betrayed spouse usually expects their wayward spouse to express guilt and remorse over the pain inflicted by the thoughtlessness of the affair, and Jon was no exception. He felt that an apology was necessary before he would be willing to reconcile. But I was able to talk him out of this condition, because I knew that at the beginning of recovery, remorse is rarely expressed. I suggested that he avoid the subject of regret unless Sue chose to express it. Instead, I wanted him to focus on what they both needed to do to meet each other's emotional needs and become more thoughtful of each other's feelings.

Sue was not unusual. It's very common for the wayward spouse to not feel remorse. And it's common for the betrayed spouse to feel that it wasn't his or her fault either. So when an affair has ended, and a couple are ready to rebuild their relationship, neither wants to take responsibility. They both see the other as having been very selfish and they see themselves as having gone the extra mile, with nothing to show for it. Why apologize for something when you feel it was the other person's fault?

I've found that an apology is not always necessary for a full marital recovery to take place after an affair. Of course, if remorse is actually felt by a spouse, I encourage that spouse to express it. I would like the wayward spouse to apologize for having betrayed a valuable trust and for having hurt in the worst way possible the very one he or she promised to love and cherish. But I would also like the betrayed spouse to apologize for having failed to meet important emotional needs that he or she had promised at the time of marriage, even if the failure was out of ignorance.

> *If the feeling of remorse is not actually felt by a spouse, I don't recommend a reluctant apology.*

If the feeling of remorse is not actually felt by a spouse, I don't recommend a reluctant apology. I don't see any sense in mouthing words that don't reflect true feelings. Insincere words won't help marital recovery. It's the new lifestyle that the couple creates that will save their marriage.

Instead of focusing their attention on the mistakes of the past, I encourage couples to focus on the present and future. They should

NOT dwell on the affair but focus on rebuilding their marriage. Every time the affair is mentioned, love units are withdrawn from both Love Banks. So the less time spent talking about the affair, the better. The couple is already painfully aware of the mistakes they made and there's no value in being reminded of what they already know.

The goal of marital recovery is to deposit enough love units for the Love Banks of both spouses to overflow. The reconciled couple must learn how to build a new lifestyle that deposits those love units and avoids their withdrawal. My plan for marital recovery helps couples learn how to create that lifestyle.

Marital Recovery after an Affair

Sue's affair with Greg and Kevin's affair with Amy were strikingly similar. They both began as a friendship and they both developed into a love relationship because important emotional needs had been met. By learning to meet each other's needs, Sue and Greg and Kevin and Amy felt they had become soul mates.

But there was one very important difference in these affairs. Sue's affair with Greg became sexual, while Kevin's never got that far. As soon as Kevin and Amy expressed their love for each other, Kevin realized that he was in trouble. He wisely confessed his feelings to Lee and ended his relationship with Amy.

> *An emotional affair can be just as much a threat to marriage as a sexual affair.*

Some would argue that Kevin never really had an affair, because they feel that a relationship outside marriage must be sexual to be considered an affair. But an emotional affair can be just as much a threat to marriage as a sexual affair. And unless Kevin had separated from Amy when he did, they would have eventually made love. I believe that anyone who is in love with someone outside of marriage, and expresses that love to him or her, is having an affair—an affair of the heart. This is particularly true when that expression of love is reciprocated.

In spite of this important difference between the two affairs—one was sexual while the other was not—my plan for marital recovery was the same for both of them. In fact the plan helps marriages recover after all types of affairs if a couple is willing to follow it. Its purpose is to rebuild Love Bank accounts and keep those accounts healthy. It's a plan to create a new lifestyle that helps a couple maintain mutual love and compatibility. It also protects a couple from a new affair.

But while the plan was the same for both couples, they began at different points on the road to recovery. Sue's affair had withdrawn so many love units from her account in Jon's Love Bank that by the time they reunited it was deeply in the red—she had a negative balance. Jon had not just stopped loving her, but he had started *disliking* her. And Jon's account in Sue's Love Bank wasn't in much better shape. Although he had tried to meet her emotional needs while she was having her affair, her love for Greg prevented Jon's care from reaching her, so none of it was recorded in her Love Bank.

Kevin and Lee, on the other hand, began their recovery with Love Bank accounts that had not taken much of a beating. The discovery of the affair was hard on Kevin's account in Lee's Love Bank, but the damage was minimized by the way he handled it—totally separating from Amy. So it was not only easier for them to follow my plan for recovery, but they saw positive results more quickly.

Since Sue and Jon had the harder and longer road to recovery, I will focus on their experience trying to follow my plan. Their reconciliation was more difficult because Sue's affair had not ended the right way—with immediate total separation from Greg after she realized she was in love with him. By pursuing the affair, Sue created many emotional obstacles to recovery. But my plan is designed to overcome even these obstacles.

By the time Sue's affair was over, and Greg was finally out of her system, she was willing to reconcile for the sake of her girls—and herself. Her daughters wanted their dad back, and with Greg out of the picture, there was no reason to keep him away. Besides, she longed to return to the days when her life was normal. Maybe having Jon home would turn the clock back to those happier days, even if she no longer felt love for Jon and had little hope of ever loving him the way she had loved Greg.

But I made it clear to Sue that Jon would only return to her on the condition that she follow my entire plan for recovery. She figured she had nothing to lose, so she agreed to follow it—at least for a while.

Jon wasn't much more enthusiastic about reconciliation. He felt like he had been through a war and didn't think he could ever trust Sue again. Jon and I had spent quite a bit of time planning for this very day, the day he would return to Sue, but Jon didn't feel like celebrating. He was, however, ready and willing to follow my plan for recovery.

Four Rules to Guide Marital Recovery

My plan to guide marital recovery after an affair is summarized in four very important rules.

The Rule of Protection: Avoid being the cause of your spouse's unhappiness.

The Rule of Care: Meet your spouse's most important emotional needs.

The Rule of Time: Take time to give your spouse undivided attention.

The Rule of Honesty: Be totally open and honest with your spouse.

Taken together these four rules create an integrated lifestyle that guarantees mutual love, and they prevent either spouse from having another affair.

Each rule is equally important, but in my plan for recovery, I help couples learn them one at a time. First, I teach the Rule of Protection because that rule prevents them from withdrawing love units from each other's Love Bank. I focus on this rule first because I want to help couples plug up the holes in their banks before they begin filling them up again. After all, why deposit love units unless you know how to avoid withdrawing them?

In the next four chapters I explain in detail how to implement these four rules, which lead to marital recovery after an affair.

Checklist for Preparing for Marital Recovery after an Affair

Getting through Withdrawal

_____ Wayward spouse should maintain total separation from the lover while getting through withdrawal symptoms.

_____ If symptoms are severe, the wayward spouse should consult with a physician for antidepressant medication.

_____ Wayward spouse should be totally honest about any contact with the lover and if contact is made, create additional precautions to ensure total separation.

What to do if the wayward spouse does not want to totally separate from the lover:

Plan A

_____ Set a time limit.

_____ Betrayed spouse should avoid angry outbursts, disrespect, and demands at all costs.

_____ Betrayed spouse should try to meet the wayward spouse's emotional needs.

Plan B

_____ Set a time limit.

_____ Betrayed spouse should arrange for friends or family to handle communication between the betrayed spouse and the wayward spouse.

_____ If there are children, the betrayed spouse should seek legal counsel regarding plans.

_____ Betrayed spouse should write and send a letter to the wayward spouse explaining plan B.

_____ After the letter is received, the betrayed spouse should avoid all contact with the wayward spouse until the affair has ended and the extraordinary measures to guarantee total separation from the lover are accepted by the wayward spouse.

_____ If there is accidental contact between the wayward spouse and betrayed spouse, the betrayed spouse should avoid angry outbursts, disrespect, and demands.

_____ Betrayed spouse should try to be surrounded by a strong and encouraging support group.

Marital Recovery Guided by
The Rule of Protection

My ultimate goal for Jon and Sue was the restoration of their love for each other. To achieve that goal, they had to redeposit all of the love units that had been withdrawn over the past two years. But before I would focus their attention on depositing those love units, I had to be sure they knew how to avoid withdrawing them.

Knowing that his wife was having an affair was the most painful experience of Jon's life, and when it was over, he had very little compassion for Sue. He wanted to have an affair himself, so she would know how it felt. He wanted to lecture her on how thoughtless she had been. He wanted to remind her of the pain he had endured. He wanted to punish her just to even the score.

Fortunately I was able to convince Jon that those instinctive responses would eventually drive Sue away from him again and make the chances of their marital recovery very unlikely. If he really wanted to save his marriage, he had to protect Sue from his negative emotional reactions—at all costs.

Even though Sue was the one who had the affair, she was also angry and resentful toward Jon. She did not welcome him home with guilt and remorse for what she had put him through. She felt that the whole ordeal was all his fault. If Jon had been looking for an apology, he came to the wrong place. Sue never did apologize.

But Sue was not only unrepentant, she was tempted to take out her anger on Jon. She had lost the one she had regarded as her soul mate for life and she somehow blamed Jon for it. Unless she were able to protect Jon from her feelings of anger, their marital recovery would end almost as quickly as it had begun.

Jon's and Sue's emotional instincts were telling them to freely express their anger and disrespect to each other. Their instincts were also encouraging them to make their decisions without considering each other's feelings. They were both hurt deeply by the events of the past two years and were very tempted to do whatever they could to make themselves feel better, even if it was at the other's expense.

If Jon and Sue were to follow the advice of their instincts, there would be no hope for marital recovery because they would be continually hurting each other. Love units would be withdrawn faster than they could ever be deposited. That's why Sue and Jon had to make a special effort to stop doing anything to hurt each other. If they didn't, whatever they would try to do to make the other happy would be wasted effort.

The first rule to guide marital recovery after an affair is the Rule of Protection: Avoid being the cause of your spouse's unhappiness. It helped remind Jon and Sue that whenever they did anything to make each other unhappy, they were withdrawing love units, making it more difficult for them to restore their love for each other.

The Rule of Protection
Avoid being the cause of your spouse's unhappiness.

The Rule of Protection highlights a very important problem that all marriages face. Instincts often encourage spouses to hurt each other, and that, in turn, destroys their love and marital happiness.

In this chapter I will begin with the more obvious ways that Jon and Sue were tempted to withdraw love units by deliberately hurting each other. Then I will describe less obvious but equally destructive ways that couples ruin their love for each other.

Love Busters: The Most Obvious Ways to Destroy Love

When Jon first counseled with me, I taught him how to follow the Rule of Protection. And he learned how to do it under the most adverse conditions—while Sue was having her affair. But I had not explained the Rule of Protection to Sue because she didn't want to talk to me while she was having her affair. So before Jon returned to her, I gave her a quick course in how to avoid hurting Jon.

I began the course with a description of the three most common Love Busters—angry outbursts, disrespectful judgments, and selfish demands. I helped Sue understand that these are Love Busters because each of them withdraws love units from her account and destroys Jon's feeling of love for her. Even though she would feel like using these Love Busters to hurt Jon, especially in the beginning of their recovery, she should do everything in her power to avoid them.

Jon also needed to be reminded to avoid Love Busters. I knew that when he and Sue got back together, there would be many occasions when he would be tempted to use them.

Angry Outbursts

Jon was very angry with the way Sue had treated him, and Sue was angry too. She felt that all of her problems were Jon's fault. If he had not left her alone so much of the time, she never would have fallen in love with Greg.

Sue and Jon needed to protect each other from their anger. If they didn't, marital recovery would be impossible.

What makes you angry? Anger usually occurs when you feel (a) that someone made you unhappy, and (b) that what they did just wasn't fair. In your angry state, you are convinced that reasoning won't work and that the offender needs to be taught a lesson. Punishment is the answer, you assume.

An angry outburst offers you a simple way to punish the troublemaker. If your spouse is the troublemaker, your anger will urge you to hurt the one you've promised to protect. Anger does not care about your spouse's feelings and is willing to scorch the culprit if it helps even the score.

In the end, you have nothing to gain from an angry outburst. Punishment does not solve marital problems; it only makes your punished spouse want to inflict punishment on you. Your spouse may rise to the challenge and try to destroy you in retaliation. When anger wins, love loses.

> **When anger wins, love loses.**

Each of us has an arsenal of weapons we use when we're angry. If we think someone deserves to be punished, we unlock the gate and select an appropriate weapon. Sometimes the weapons are verbal (ridicule and sarcasm), sometimes they're devious plots to cause suffering, and sometimes they're physical. But they all have one thing in common: They're intended to hurt people. Since our partner is at such close range, we can use our weapons to hurt him or her the most.

Some of the husbands and wives I've counseled have fairly harmless arsenals, maybe just a few awkward efforts at ridicule. Others are armed to nuclear proportions, actually putting their spouse's life in danger. The more dangerous your weapons are, the more important it is to control your temper. If you've ever lost your temper in a way that has caused your spouse great pain and suffering, you know that you cannot afford to lose your temper again. You must go to extreme lengths to protect your spouse from yourself.

Remember, in marriage you can be your spouse's greatest source of pleasure, but you can also be your spouse's greatest source of pain, particularly when he or she receives the brunt of your angry outburst.

It was easy for Jon and Sue to begin blaming each other for the nightmare they had experienced because they were both upset with each other. And it was difficult to keep their arsenals of weapons locked up. But by agreeing to avoid angry outbursts, they avoided one of the most dangerous threats to their marital recovery.

Disrespectful Judgments

Jon did a good job controlling his temper but he had more difficulty being respectful to Sue after what she'd put him through. It was all he could do to avoid lecturing her on the consequences of her shortsighted and thoughtless ways. After all, her life was in ruins after the affair was over. If Jon had not graciously come back to her to give their marriage another chance, it would have remained in ruins. Jon wanted to be sure that Sue had learned a lesson from it all.

But Sue didn't feel she had much to learn at all. She felt that it was Jon who had lessons to learn, and no amount of lecturing on his part would have changed her mind. It would have only infuriated her.

Have you ever tried to "straighten out" someone? We're all occasionally tempted to do it. We usually think we're doing that person a big favor, lifting him or her from the darkness of confusion into the light of our superior perspective. If people would only follow our advice, we assume, they could avoid many of life's pitfalls.

But if you ever try to straighten out your spouse, to keep him or her from making mistakes, you are making a much bigger mistake. I call it a disrespectful judgment, and your disrespectful judgment withdraws love units, destroying love.

> *A disrespectful judgment occurs whenever someone tries to impose a system of values and beliefs on someone else.*

A disrespectful judgment occurs whenever someone tries to impose a system of values and beliefs on someone else. When a husband tries to force his point of view on his wife, he's just asking for trouble. When a wife assumes that her own views are right and her husband is woefully misguided—and tells him so—she enters a minefield.

Trouble starts when you think you have the right—even the responsibility—to impose your view on your spouse. Almost invariably, he or she will regard such imposition as personally threatening, arrogant, rude, and incredibly disrespectful. That's when you lose love units in your spouse's Love Bank.

When you try to impose your opinions on your spouse, you imply that he or she has poor judgment. That's disrespectful. You may not say this in so many words, but it's the clear message that your spouse hears. If you value your spouse's judgment, you won't be so quick to discard his or her opinions. You will consider the possibility that your spouse may be right and you wrong.

I'm not saying that you can't disagree with your spouse. But you should disagree *respectfully.* Try to understand your spouse's perspective. Present the information that brought you to your opinion and listen to the information he or she brings. Entertain the possibility of changing your mind, instead of just trying to change your spouse's mind.

You see, each of us brings two things into a marriage—wisdom and foolishness. A marriage thrives when a husband and wife can blend their value systems, with each one's wisdom overriding the other's foolishness. By sharing their ideas and sorting through the pros and cons, a couple can create a belief system superior to what either partner had alone. But unless they approach the task with mutual respect—using respectful persuasion—the process won't work and they'll destroy their love for each other.

Respectful persuasion works like this: You begin by respecting the belief your spouse already has and understanding why your spouse believes it. Then you suggest an alternative belief that you think will be in your spouse's best interest and not just in your own best interest. Finally, if your spouse is willing, you may need to do a test to prove your point. This may allow your spouse to see how useful the alternative belief can be. But in the final analysis, regardless of your evidence, the choice to change beliefs should be completely up to your spouse.

Imagine yourself as a refrigerator salesperson. How should you go about convincing a couple to buy your refrigerator? Would you go to their house, take one look at their refrigerator, and tell them that it's a piece of junk? Would that land you a sale? Not very likely. Instead, you and all your brochures would probably be thrown out of the house.

If you really wanted to make a sale, you would first try to understand your customers' needs. Then, without criticizing their refrigerator, you would explain the benefits of your refrigerator and how it would meet those needs. You would let the couple decide whether the benefits you present would make buying a new refrigerator worthwhile. Then, if they decided to keep their existing refrigerator, you would respect that decision so that some day, when they had a change of heart, the couple might buy their next one from you.

Respectful persuasion doesn't guarantee that you will win over your spouse to your opinion. It does guarantee, however, that you won't alienate him or her with your arrogant tactics.

When Sue asked Jon to come home, she wasn't inviting him to lecture her or to try to straighten her out. She did not want Jon to remind her of the mistakes she had made. She wanted to give their marriage a fresh start and she wanted to be convinced that Jon would help her create a better marriage. So it was important for Jon to understand that he had to avoid anything that Sue would interpret as a disrespectful judgment. To help him out, Sue gladly offered to bring instances of his disrespect to his attention. Whenever she did, he apologized. Sue agreed to do the same when Jon felt she was being disrespectful of him.

Selfish Demands

When Jon returned to Sue, he really didn't feel like doing much for her. He felt she should repay him for everything she'd put him through. But Sue didn't feel like doing much for Jon, either. With both of them feeling that the other person had lots of making up to do, they were both tempted to make demands of each other. I warned them that demands were another Love Buster, and if they tried using it, they would have a much more difficult time restoring love to their marriage.

Our parents made demands on us when we were children; teachers made demands on us in school; and employers make demands at work. Most of us didn't like them as children, and we still don't.

Demands carry a threat of punishment. *If you refuse me, you'll regret it.* In other words, you may dislike doing what I want, but if you don't do it, I'll see to it that you suffer even greater pain.

People who make demands don't seem to care how others feel. They think only of their own needs. *If you find it unpleasant to do what I want, tough! And if you refuse, I'll make it even tougher.*

Demands depend on power. They don't work unless the demanding one has the power to make good on the threats. But in a marriage, there should be shared power—the husband and wife working together to accomplish mutual objectives with mutual agreement. When one spouse starts making demands—along with threats that are at least implied—power is no longer shared. As a result, the threatened spouse often strikes back, fighting fire with fire, power with power. Suddenly the marriage is a tug-of-war instead of a bicycle built for two. It's a test of strength—who has enough power to win? When one spouse wins and the other loses, the marriage loses.

> When one spouse wins and the other loses, the marriage loses.

Demands are the wrong way to get what you need from each other. When you ask your spouse to do something for you, he or she may cheerfully agree to do it or may express reluctance. This reluctance may be due to any number of causes—personal needs, comfort level, a sense of what's wise or fair. But be assured that there is a reason for reluctance, and from your spouse's viewpoint, it's a good reason.

If after your spouse expresses reluctance, you insist on your request, making it a demand, what are you doing? You are declaring that your wishes are more important than his or her feelings. And you are threatening a distressful outcome if your demands are not met.

Now your spouse must choose the lesser of the two evils—your "punishment" on the one hand or his or her cause for reluctance on the other. Your spouse may ultimately submit to your demand, and you get your way but it will be at your spouse's expense. I guarantee you, your spouse will feel used, and rightfully so. And you will withdraw love units in the process.

Sometimes a wife says, *But you don't know my husband! He lies around the house all night, and I can't get him to do a thing. The only time he lifts a finger is to press the remote control. If I don't demand that he get up and help me, nothing will get done.*

Requests don't work with my wife, a husband might say. *She only thinks about herself! She spends her whole life shopping and going out with her girlfriends. If I didn't demand that she stay at home once in a while, I'd never see her.*

My answer is that demands are an ineffective way to get a husband to help around the house or to keep a wife from going out with her friends. Demands do not encourage people to cooperate; they only withdraw love units. If you force your spouse to meet your needs, it becomes a temporary solution at best, and resentment is sure to rear its ugly head. Threats, lectures, and other forms of manipulation do not build compatibility—they build resentment.

Thoughtless Decisions: A Less Obvious Way to Destroy Love

Sue agreed with me that angry outbursts, disrespectful judgments, and selfish demands should be avoided. And as long as Jon was willing to protect her from those three Love Busters, she was willing to protect him from them too.

But Jon's and Sue's protection of each other had to go beyond just avoiding those Love Busters—it had to reach out to almost everything they did. That's because almost everything they did affected each other. Some of their habits and activities had a positive effect and made each other happy. But other habits and activities had a negative effect—they caused each other to be unhappy.

Each decision that Sue and Jon made resulted in either the deposit or withdrawal of love units. That awareness was a major awakening for both of them. Sue saw for the first time that if she were to protect Jon, she could no longer make decisions without first considering how they would affect him. If a decision would make him unhappy, she would be violating my first rule to guide marital recovery, the Rule of Protection.

Many of Jon's and Sue's decisions that had caused each other's unhappiness were innocent. They had not realized they were thoughtless. For example, Jon's time spent away from his family developing a career was thoughtless because it had made Sue feel very unhappy. But Jon did it in an effort to provide his family with a higher standard of living. Jon thought Sue appreciated his hard work, but she actually resented it and it became a major cause of withdrawals from his account in her Love Bank.

I gave Jon and Sue a way to avoid the risk of making thoughtless decisions. It's called the Policy of Joint Agreement: Never do anything without an enthusiastic agreement between you and your spouse.

The Policy of Joint Agreement

Never do anything without an enthusiastic agreement between you and your spouse.

This policy unmasks thoughtless decisions because it identifies habits and activities that have the potential to cause unhappiness. If Sue and Jon were willing to avoid being the cause of each other's unhappiness, they had to talk about the things they planned to do and hear each other's feelings about those plans. The Policy of Joint Agreement simply took their willingness to protect each other a step further. It eliminated habits and activities that seemed innocent at the time, but would have caused either of them to be unhappy.

Thoughtfulness: The Objective of Marital Negotiation

Jon and Sue both agreed with me that they needed to stop making decisions that were good for one and bad for the other. They agreed that the gains from having a mutually agreeable lifestyle more than outweighed the personal loss of making independent decisions. They learned to ask each other *How would you feel?* before they made any decision.

That's the first step toward marital negotiation—asking the question, "How would you feel?" Without it couples don't negotiate. They simply make their decisions without regard for each other's feelings. But following the Policy of Joint Agreement guaranteed that Sue and Jon would negotiate, because they couldn't do anything until they were both in agreement. The Policy of Joint Agreement changed the way they discussed issues, and for the first time in their marriage, they were communicating with the deepest concern for each other's feelings.

In most marriages, negotiation is tough. Whenever there is a conflict of opinions, spouses usually either do whatever they're asked or refuse to do much of anything. Discussing each conflict until a mutually enthusiastic agreement is reached is very unusual. But that's because most spouses are unskilled in negotiating with each other. They don't know how to work out agreements that are in their mutual interest.

> *If a couple are committed to avoid any decision until they come to a mutually enthusiastic agreement, eventually they learn how to negotiate.*

However, if a couple are committed to avoid any decision until they come to a mutually enthusiastic agreement, eventually they learn how to negotiate, and they do it almost effortlessly. They become very creative in discovering solutions to problems and this leads to their mutual happiness.

The Policy of Joint Agreement forced Jon and Sue to negotiate until they could arrive at a decision that would not hurt either of them. It forced them to be thoughtful. These mutually acceptable decisions formed the foundation for a new lifestyle that they would share with each other—a lifestyle that would not withdraw love units from either of their Love Banks.

How to Negotiate with the Policy of Joint Agreement

Throughout Sue and Jon's marriage the issue of his business travel had been a source of unhappiness for Sue. She was lonely when he was away from home. Now Jon had a new position that didn't require traveling, but it paid quite a bit less, and they both missed his higher income. Sue wanted Jon's previous income without the problems his travel caused. Jon and Sue needed to find a solution to this dilemma, so it was on this issue that I taught them to negotiate with the Policy of Joint Agreement.

There are four guidelines that I recommend to couples for reaching an enthusiastic agreement. I encouraged Jon and Sue to use them as they discussed his career alternatives.

Guideline 1. *Set ground rules to make negotiations pleasant and safe.*

Before you start to negotiate, agree with each other that you will both follow these rules: (a) be pleasant and cheerful throughout your discussion of the issue; (b) put safety first—do not threaten to cause pain or suffering when you negotiate, even if your negotiations fail; and (c) if you reach an impasse, stop for a while and come back to the issue later.

One spouse's negative comment or pessimistic attitude will often trigger an escalation of negativity and pessimism from the other spouse. This can lead to Love Busters intruding on your happy conversation. Angry outbursts, disrespectful judgments, and selfish demands will ruin any effort you make to negotiate. You will simply never have an enthusiastic agreement about anything if you hurt each other as you try to solve your problems. Instead, try your best to soothe each other when something said creates a negative reaction.

> *If your negotiation becomes unpleasant or unsafe to either of you, break it off and choose another time to discuss the issue.*

If your negotiation becomes unpleasant or unsafe to either of you, break it off and choose another time to discuss the issue. Do the same thing if it appears you have reached an impasse. Taking a break will allow tempers to cool, and may reveal new insights that can be discussed when you begin your negotiations again.

Guideline 2. *Identify the problem from the perspectives of both you and your spouse.*

Be able to state each other's position on the issue before you go on to find a solution. Each of you should describe what you would like and why you would like it. Then explain the other's position to each other's satisfaction. Be sure you fully understand each other before you go any further toward an agreement. And respect your differences of opinion.

As soon as Sue began to explain how she felt about Jon's trips away from home, she could hardly hold back her tears. She explained how she had wanted Jon to reach his highest potential with his job and earn a living that would create a comfortable lifestyle for their family. Yet, whenever he was gone, she felt very lonely, as if he had abandoned her. She explained that while her needs were not being met when he traveled, her need for financial support was not being met by his new position that did not require travel. She wanted to find a solution that would enable him to meet all of her emotional needs.

After Sue explained her perspective, Jon summarized what he heard. He tried to put into his own words what Sue felt. When he was finished, Sue made a few minor corrections to clarify her perspective but in general was very pleased with Jon's summary and felt that he understood her position.

Then Jon described his perspective. He began by explaining how they had been living above their means for some time. Before the affair they had spent just about everything he earned. But during their separation their expenses skyrocketed. Jon had to borrow heavily to pay his own living expenses and pay the support to Sue that the court had ordered. It had left them on the verge of bankruptcy.

To add to this financial crisis, Jon had given up his high-paying position to take a lower-paying position that did not require travel. He did this while Sue was having her affair as an expression of his willingness and ability to meet her emotional needs when she would return to him.

After hearing Jon's perspective, Sue summarized what she heard. Jon was satisfied that it accurately reflected his feelings.

This was not the first time they had this conversation. But they had never gone beyond that second step of understanding each other's perspective. They knew what the problem was but they had never solved it. They had not used the Policy of Joint Agreement to guide them toward a solution. Now their financial crisis pushed them to the fast track toward a solution to the problem. They had to come quickly to an enthusiastic agreement.

Guideline 3. *Brainstorm solutions with abandon.*

Give your brains the opportunity to do what they do best—solve problems. Think of all sorts of possible solutions and write them all down. Don't criticize an option that you don't like—you'll have a chance to evaluate the choices when you come to the fourth guideline. If you use your imaginations, you will have a long list of ideas to consider.

Jon and Sue came up with these possible solutions:

a. Jon tries to find a higher paying job that does not require travel.
b. Jon stays in his current position that does not require travel. They adjust to his lower salary by lowering their standard of living, selling their home, and buying a more affordable home.
c. Jon stays in his current position and Sue works full-time to help pay off the debt and compensate for Jon's lower income.
d. Jon returns to his old position, but Sue travels with him—leaving the children with friends or family.
e. Jon returns to his old position until their debt is eliminated, but they live under a strict budget that would have their bills

paid in two years. Whenever he travels, each day he calls Sue at least three times, engages in at least one and a half hours of conversation, and faxes her a letter. He gives her flowers before he leaves, brings her a gift when he returns, and goes away alone with Sue for a weekend after each trip. He limits his trips to only three nights away from home.

The longer they thought about the issues, the more creative they became. I encouraged them both to let their minds run wild and write down anything they wanted. Jon suggested that he quit his job and that they all join the Peace Corps. Sue didn't criticize his idea. Instead, she just smiled.

Guideline 4. *Choose a solution that is appealing to both of you.*
From your list of possible solutions, many will satisfy only one of you. However, scattered within the list will be solutions that both of you may find attractive. Among those solutions that are mutually satisfactory, select the one that you both like the most as the final solution to your problem. But if you can't find one that you can both agree to enthusiastically, go back to guideline 3 and brainstorm some more.

Before choosing a final solution, Jon and Sue took several days gathering information. Jon discovered that his old position, with its increased salary, was available to him if he wanted it back. Sue confirmed that her responsibilities at work were flexible and that she could join Jon on business trips once in a while. He also made a few telephone calls to see if he could work for another company in a position that did not require as much travel.

In the end, they enthusiastically agreed to a solution that combined several of their ideas. Their ultimate goal was for Jon to have a job that would decrease their debt yet give the family a high quality of life. That quality of life was to include Jon's ability to meet Sue's emotional needs, not leaving her feeling lonely when he had to travel.

Sue felt that she could often travel with Jon. When she couldn't, he would follow the terms of idea e. He would call her several times a day and when he returned they would spend a weekend together by themselves.

They made up a budget, assigning part of Jon's income to pay off their debt. But the added cost of Sue traveling with Jon would prevent them from paying it off in two years, as they would have liked.

Both Jon and Sue were finally enthusiastic about the solution to their problem.

Some marital conflicts are as difficult to solve as Jon's travel problem. But most of them are relatively easy to solve. If you begin with an understanding that a solution cannot be chosen until you have enthusiastic agreement, you will be amazed at how quickly you can find agreement. The solutions were there all along, but you had just never looked for them before.

> *If you begin with an understanding that a solution cannot be chosen until you have enthusiastic agreement, you will be amazed at how quickly you can find agreement.*

At first, to find a solution to their conflicts, Jon and Sue had to sit down and formally follow the four guidelines I had given them. But the more they practiced, the easier it was for them to come to an enthusiastic agreement, and following the guidelines seemed to come naturally.

Negotiating on the Run

Most marital decisions are not made with calm deliberation. While brainstorming alternatives over a cup of coffee might be the most desirable way to solve problems, in practice, couples need to develop skill in making thoughtful decisions on the run.

So after Jon and Sue had practiced negotiating with the four guidelines I had proposed, I encouraged them to adapt the same guidelines to decisions they made when they were pressed for time. They had a chance to test their skills one Saturday afternoon as they were shopping for new tennis shoes.

As they approached the shoe store they came upon a sidewalk sale—one of Jon's worst nightmares. Sue stopped to look at the clearance tables and spent the next thirty minutes sorting through the bargains.

Jon reminded Sue that they had promised the baby-sitter they would be home by 3:00. Sue went right to a pay phone to tell the baby-sitter that they would be a little late. Jon was not happy with the way the events developed but he didn't know how to explain it to Sue.

Their problem was that Sue had not asked how Jon would feel about taking time to look at the bargains on the sidewalk. And Jon had not let Sue know that it was not the baby-sitter that bothered him; it was her taking the time to shop for bargains. They forgot to use the Policy of Joint Agreement and as a result, they had an unpleasant experience together.

It takes a while to develop the skill of constantly using the Policy of Joint Agreement to make decisions. I recommend to couples that they choose a simple phrase to help express their feelings when negotiation is needed—something like, *Will you negotiate with me about this?* This serves as a reminder that no decision should be made without the enthusiastic agreement of both of them. Then, if possible, I have them negotiate "on the run."

Let me show you how this would have worked in Jon and Sue's shopping experience.

Jon sees the endless rows of tables as they enter the mall. He immediately feels anxiety and discomfort because he knows how much Sue loves to shop and how he hates to wait for her. As Sue starts looking at the tables, Jon could say, *Honey, I'm not very enthusiastic about this situation. Will you negotiate with me?* Sue stops looking at the sale items, and spends a few minutes considering alternatives. They briefly share their perspectives on the problem without being defensive or demanding and throw out a few possible solutions. They finally agree that Jon will go right to the shoe store, and Sue will meet him there fifteen minutes later. Conflict resolved!

> *I highly recommend to couples that they learn to say something like,* I'm not very enthusiastic about this situation, will you negotiate with me?

But shouldn't Sue have asked him how he felt about her shopping before she actually started looking at the sale tables? Ideally, yes. But in practice, couples don't always know how each other feels about things, and it often doesn't occur to them to ask. In this example, Sue thought she would spend only a few minutes looking at the sale items and didn't know that Jon would be upset. He had to tell her. But then, once she knew how he felt, the Rule of Protection—*avoid being the cause of your spouse's unhappiness*—would have guided her response. She would have stopped in her tracks and negotiated a resolution to the problem. The Policy of Joint Agreement would then have guided them to a solution that would have saved the afternoon.

I highly recommend to couples that they learn to say something like, *I'm not very enthusiastic about this situation, will you negotiate with me?* It may feel strange at first, as if you are speaking a new language. But there are many advantages to it. The phrase is a gentle reminder to your spouse that you have both agreed to follow the Policy of Joint Agreement, and it keeps you from saying something hurtful out of frustration. By expressing your unhappiness through a sentence you've both agreed to, you trigger a mutual effort to reach an enthusiastic agreement.

The Policy of Joint Agreement Offers Complete Protection

The Policy of Joint Agreement is nothing more than a reminder to be thoughtful. Almost everything one spouse does in some way affects the other spouse. If you have habits that hurt each other, those habits can become excruciatingly painful. You can become your spouse's greatest source of unhappiness unless you deliberately protect your spouse from your thoughtless behavior. So it makes sense to ask, *How do you feel about what I do?*

If something you want to do is not agreeable to your spouse, the Policy of Joint Agreement offers your spouse protection. Following the Policy means that if something you want to do very much would hurt your spouse, you won't do it.

The Policy of Joint Agreement encourages couples to consider each other's happiness as important as their own. When one spouse considers his or her own interests so important that he or she tramples over the interests of the other, it's a formula for marital disaster, and yet some of the most well-intentioned couples do it regularly. It's difficult to be thoughtful when it means we won't get what we want.

This Policy provides protection from such self-centeredness. It forces a couple to take each other's feelings into account with *every* decision and *every* behavior. By following the Policy, a couple makes all of their decisions together, and they avoid final choices until there is an enthusiastic agreement. In this way they build a partnership that will last for life.

The Policy of Joint Agreement Creates a Compatible Lifestyle

Building a marital relationship is like building a house—brick by brick. Each brick is a choice you make about the way you live together. If you follow the Policy of Joint Agreement and make choices that are mutually agreeable, your house will be strong and beautiful. But if some bricks are made by only one of you, those weak bricks will make your whole house an uncomfortable place to live.

When couples follow the Policy of Joint Agreement, they gradually throw out all their thoughtless habits and activities and replace them with habits and activities that take each other's feelings into account. That's what compatibility is all about—building a way of life that is comfortable for both spouses. When a couple create a lifestyle that they each enjoy and appreciate, they build compatibility into their marriage.

Compatibility means that you live in harmony with each other. It means enjoying the lifestyle you created because it is what both of you want and need. Each brick that goes into your house is there because you are both comfortable with it.

> *When a couple create a lifestyle that they each enjoy and appreciate, they build compatibility into their marriage.*

Incompatibility, on the other hand, is created when the Policy of Joint Agreement is not followed—when one spouse adds bricks that may be in his or her own best interest but are not in the other's best interest. Incompatibility, therefore, is simply the accumulation of thoughtless habits and activities. The more of them a couple try to tolerate, the more incompatible they become.

Jon and Sue had failed to take each other's feelings into account when making daily decisions. They had built their marriage with independent decisions that created independent lifestyles. Their independence led to an environment that made Sue's affair possible—bricks that threatened to destroy their house.

You Can Be the Greatest Cause of Your Spouse's Unhappiness

The skill that Jon and Sue developed as negotiators helped make their marriage safe. They learned how to avoid being the cause of each other's unhappiness. Granted, they needed to do more than make each other safe, but that first objective was crucial to achieving any of the other objectives. Without safety, any effort to find marital fulfillment is wasted. You cannot expect to meet your spouse's emotional needs until you have first learned to protect him or her from your selfish instincts. You can't expect to accumulate love units until you learn to avoid withdrawing them. If you don't develop skills of protection, you cannot expect your spouse to love you.

If you have difficulty controlling your Love Busters—angry outbursts, disrespectful judgments, or selfish demands—I suggest a book I've written that will guide you toward a safer marriage. It is *Love Busters: Overcoming Habits That Destroy Romantic Love.* In this book I help expose the destructiveness of angry outbursts, disrespectful judgments, and selfish demands. Then I show you how to overcome them so that Love Busters no longer ruin the safety of your marriage.

If you need help learning how to negotiate, I recommend *Give & Take: The Secret to Marital Compatibility.* In this book I explain why negotiation in marriage is so important, and how you can learn to apply the Policy of Joint Agreement to each decision you make in your marriage to create a loving and compatible relationship.

By resolving their conflicts with mutual protection in mind, Sue and Jon were already feeling closer to each other. They had created a plan regarding Jon's traveling that encouraged both of them and they were learning how to negotiate on the run. As a result they felt protected and safe. That, in turn, gave them the courage to become more vulnerable to each other and allow their emotional needs to be met.

Checklist for Following the Rule of Protection:
Avoid Being the Cause of Your Spouse's Unhappiness

_____ Avoid Love Busters to prevent obvious harm:

     _____ Avoid angry outbursts.

     _____ Avoid disrespectful judgments.

     _____ Avoid selfish demands.

     _____ Read *Love Busters: Overcoming Habits That Destroy Romantic Love* if help is needed to avoid Love Busters.

_____ Follow the Policy of Joint Agreement (never do anything without an enthusiastic agreement between you and your spouse) to prevent less obvious harm.

_____ Learn to negotiate with the Policy of Joint Agreement:

     _____ Guideline 1: Set ground rules to make negotiation pleasant and safe.

     _____ Guideline 2: Identify problem from the perspective of both spouses.

     _____ Guideline 3: Brainstorm solutions with abandon.

     _____ Guideline 4: Choose a solution that is appealing to both spouses.

_____ Learn to negotiate on the run:

     _____ Get into the habit of asking *How would you feel?* before making a decision or plan.

     _____ If one spouse forgets to follow the Policy of Joint Agreement, the other spouse should use a nonthreatening reminder such as, *Honey, I'm not enthusiastic about this situation. Will you negotiate with me?*

_____ Read *Give and Take: The Secret to Marital Compatibility* if help is needed to negotiate with the Policy of Joint Agreement.

MARITAL RECOVERY GUIDED BY
THE RULE OF CARE

The Rule of Protection guided Sue and Jon away from their instinct to hurt each other at a time when they were very upset. If they had not made an effort to avoid it, they would have both blamed each other for the mess they were in. Any hope for a recovery would have been blown away by their thoughtlessness.

But Sue and Jon committed themselves to the Rule of Protection. They avoided angry outbursts, disrespectful judgments, and selfish demands, and they followed the Policy of Joint Agreement so that they would avoid making thoughtless decisions.

That's why a couple recovering from the ravages of an affair must first focus their attention on protection. Their relationship is usually so fragile that they must be careful not to make matters worse by hurting each other.

But thoughtlessness isn't really what got Sue and Jon into trouble in the first place. It was the failure to meet important emotional needs. More to the point, it was Jon's failure to meet Sue's important emotional needs that was the core of their problem. Now they were ready to solve the problem—they were ready to learn about the second rule to guide marital recovery, the Rule of Care: Meet your spouse's most important emotional needs.

The Rule of Care
Meet your spouse's most important emotional needs.

Care is a word with many meanings in our language. When we say we care, it can mean that we are concerned about someone and hope that person will be happy in life. It can also mean that we have strong emotional feelings for the person.

But I use the word *care* to mean what we *do* for each other, not how we *feel*. Care, to me, is meeting important emotional needs. When, during their wedding ceremony, Jon promised that he would care for Sue, he promised to meet her most important emotional needs. But his career got in the way. As his work consumed an increasing amount of his time and energy, he no longer provided the kind of care for Sue that she needed the most—he failed to meet some of her most important emotional needs.

Quite innocently Jon had failed to meet Sue's need for conversation. Jon was away from home so much of the time that Sue had developed interests that were completely independent of Jon. This made what brief conversations they had superficial because they had grown apart from each other and had few experiences in common.

Jon also failed to meet Sue's need for admiration. Before her affair, he had little idea of how she spent her time. He didn't know about the success she was having with the children she taught at school. He didn't know about her recommendations that had been approved by the Lake Restoration Committee. He was unable to admire Sue's achievements as he had in the past and support her in her efforts. He just didn't know about them. He had lost his ability to be her best friend, the one who would be there when she needed him the most, the one to whom she could talk about the significant events of her life. And in Jon's absence, Greg stepped in.

Infidelity and multiple marriages represent ways to adjust to the failure to have emotional needs met in marriage. Over a period of time, as needs go unmet and a relationship falls apart, a new relationship may be created with another individual who satisfies the unmet needs. But learning to meet each other's emotional needs in marriage is far less complicated than going through the agonizing ritual of affairs and divorce. And learning to meet emotional needs is the solution to marital problems, while affairs and divorce make a solution impossible.

> Learning to meet each other's emotional needs in marriage is far less complicated than going through the agonizing ritual of affairs and divorce.

Jon and Sue had no difficulty understanding the importance of the Rule of Care. They both saw how Jon's career had stunted the growth of their relationship and had almost killed it. They were ready to solve the problem that had almost ended their marriage. They were ready to follow the Rule of Care.

I presented the Rule of Care to Sue and Jon in two parts. The first part of the rule is knowing which emotional needs should be met. The second part of the rule is becoming an expert at meeting those needs.

The Rule of Care, Step 1—Identify the Most Important Emotional Needs

Before Sue and Jon could care for each other effectively, they had to know where to put their effort. So their first step was to identify their own most important emotional needs.

Do you know yourself well enough to list your most important emotional needs? Most people haven't given this much thought, and if forced to make up a list, they would not know where to begin. But it's very important that you understand your needs, not only for your own sake, but for the sake of your spouse. If he or she is going to put time and energy into becoming an expert at meeting those needs, you'd better be sure you've identified the right ones. And it's also important for you to understand your spouse's emotional needs so that you can put your effort in the right place.

When I first understood the importance of emotional needs in creating love, I asked each spouse I counseled to identify what his or her spouse could do to make them the happiest. Their answers helped me identify ten emotional needs so powerful that when met by someone of the opposite sex, the feeling of love is created. I listed these ten emotional needs in chapter 3; they are affection, sexual fulfillment, conversation, recreational companionship, honesty and openness, physical attractiveness, financial support, domestic support, family commitment, and admiration. When these needs are met in marriage, people experience great pleasure, and when they are not met, they experience great frustration and disappointment.

While almost everyone has these ten needs to some extent, the importance of each need varies greatly from person to person. Some people feel a great deal of pleasure when the need for affection is met. Others don't feel much at all when affection is given. The same can be said for admiration; some need it greatly, while others don't. The same is also true for all the other emotional needs.

So while this list identifies the most common important emotional needs, all ten are not usually important for any one person. In fact I've found that, in general, only five out of the ten identified by a person have the potential for depositing enough love units to create the feeling of love.

Since not all needs are equally important, it isn't necessary to meet all ten needs in marriage. If a spouse simply learns to meet the five given highest priority, he or she will deposit enough love units to sustain romantic love. To a great extent, trying to meet the other needs would be a waste of time and energy.

Which are the most important to you? Which are the most important to your spouse? It's very likely that the ones you pick will not be exactly the same as the ones your spouse picks. They may even be entirely different.

As I said earlier, men and women tend to prioritize these ten needs very differently. Men tend to give highest priority to:

1. sexual fulfillment
2. recreational companionship
3. physical attractiveness
4. domestic support
5. admiration

Women, on the other hand, tend to give the highest priority to:

1. affection
2. conversation
3. honesty and openness
4. financial support
5. family commitment

Of course, not every man would pick the five needs I listed for men. Nor would every woman pick the five needs listed for women. Some men would include affection and conversation in their top five needs, and some women rank admiration and sexual fulfillment among their most important needs. But on average, I've found that men and women rank these needs the way I listed them.

Since the way men and women tend to prioritize their needs is so different, it's no wonder they have difficulty adjusting in marriage! A man can set out to meet his wife's needs but he will fail miserably if he assumes that her needs are the same as his. A woman will also fail if she assumes her husband has the same needs as she has.

I have seen this simple error threaten many marriages. A husband and wife fail to meet each other's needs—not because they're selfish or uncaring, but because they are ignorant of what those needs are.

She may think that showering him with love notes and affection will please him, because it pleases her. He thinks that he is doing her a big favor by inviting her to play golf, because he would be thrilled by the offer. Both partners think they are valiantly trying to meet each other's needs, but they may be aiming at the wrong target.

So, where should you put your greatest effort so that you can deposit the most love units? Meet each other's *most important* emotional needs.

How can you discover which needs are the most important to each of you? Ask.

> You must ask if you want to know where to put your greatest effort.

As I've explained, you cannot assume that your spouse's needs will be the same as yours. You are the only one who can identify your most important emotional needs, and your spouse is the best expert on his or her needs. You must ask if you want to know where to put your greatest effort.

The ten needs that I focus attention on do not exhaust the list of possible needs. Other needs such as ambition—when a spouse achieves important objectives—could be included on your list if they are important to you. This will require you to identify them yourself, from your past experiences. Think about what makes you the happiest, then the times when these needs were met will come to mind, and you will be able to identify them. For most of us, though, the ten needs that I listed cover the bases.

Listing Your Most Important Emotional Needs

I have made it easy for you and your spouse to identify for each other your most important emotional needs. To help you understand your choices, I have described each of the ten most important emotional needs in appendix A. Read each carefully.

Then, after you have been introduced to the ten needs, complete the Emotional Needs Questionnaire I have provided for you in appendix B. Make two enlarged copies of this questionnaire so both you and your spouse can complete one of them.

Remember how I described an emotional need in chapter 3? It is a craving that when satisfied leaves you feeling happy and content, and when unsatisfied leaves you unhappy and frustrated. The word *craving* is an important part of that definition. If you have a craving for any of the possible needs, it should be on your list of most important emotional needs.

When you come to the last page of the questionnaire, where you are asked to rank your needs according to their importance to you, consider the following—If you don't choose sexual fulfillment as a most important need, imagine never having sex with your spouse. If you don't choose affection, imagine your spouse never expressing his or her love for you—no hugs, no kisses, no love notes. If you don't choose financial support, imagine your spouse not earning a dime throughout your life together.

To help you rank your needs, imagine your spouse meeting only one of the ten needs and failing to meet the other nine. Under that condition, which would give you the most satisfaction and the least frustration? Which would deposit the most love units? You should rank that need number 1. Continue this imagining process until you have identified the five emotional needs that mean the most to you.

Before you leave this assignment, give your list of five needs one last look and give special attention to those you didn't include. If all five of the needs you've listed are met by your spouse, will you be happy? If your spouse fails to meet a need that is not included on your list, will it threaten to ruin your marriage? If there is a sixth need that you feel must be included to ensure the success of your marriage, add it to the list. But then let your spouse also add a sixth need to his or her list.

My experience with most couples shows that the higher the ranking, the more effort should be given to meeting that need. In some cases an outstanding job meeting the top two needs is all it takes to deposit enough love units to trigger the feeling of love. If a reasonably good effort is made to meet the other three, it just adds insurance to the Love Bank account. But couples who try to meet all ten needs, try to do too much and usually do a poor or mediocre job on all of them. In those marriages, even though a great deal of effort is made, the results are very disappointing. Couples who focus their attention on each other's top five emotional needs have a sensational marriage.

> Couples who focus their attention on each other's top five emotional needs have a sensational marriage.

It's safe to assume that the needs you and your spouse ranked number 1 and number 2 should get your very special attention. But don't ignore the other three. If you leave any of the top five needs unmet in your marriage, your love for each other will be at risk and your spouse will be vulnerable to an outside person meeting those needs. Recovery from an affair depends on each spouse being an expert at meeting the other's top five needs—especially the top two.

Jon and Sue Rank Their Needs

I asked Jon and Sue to do what I just suggested you and your spouse do—identify the most important emotional needs. First, they became familiar with the ten emotional needs and then they both completed the Emotional Needs Questionnaire.

Sue ranked her top five emotional needs as follows:

1. conversation
2. affection
3. admiration
4. financial support
5. family commitment

Sue's list helped Jon see why his job had almost ruined their marriage. His financial support was important to her because it met one of her most important emotional needs. But in meeting that need for financial support, he had failed to meet three needs that were more important to her—the needs for conversation, affection, and admiration. The time he had taken to earn more money prevented him from meeting those more important emotional needs.

Jon's list of important emotional needs was very different than Sue's. He ranked his needs this way:

1. sexual fulfillment
2. physical attractiveness
3. honesty and openness
4. domestic support
5. recreational companionship

Sue had done a terrific job meeting Jon's need for sexual fulfillment. Even after she began to feel less enthusiastic about making love to Jon, he didn't know about her loss of passion, except for that one fateful evening on their eighth wedding anniversary. But after that, she never denied him sex and often approached him when she thought he would like it. Because it was his most important emotional need, in meeting that need Sue continued to deposit more than enough love units for him to be in love with her.

But she did even more for him. She was physically attractive to him, she did a great job managing the home and taking care of their children, and when he had a break in his work schedule, she often joined him in *his* favorite recreational activities. The only need she had failed to meet was his need for honesty and openness. And he didn't know she was being dishonest until her affair had already begun. From Jon's perspective, Sue had been the perfect wife.

But from Sue's perspective, Jon had a lot to learn.

The Rule of Care, Step 2—Become an Expert at Meeting the Most Important Emotional Needs

Most of our happiness in life comes from our relationships with others. That's because we can't meet our most important emotional needs ourselves—others must meet them for us. And we usually fall in love with and marry the person we think will do the very best job meeting them.

> *We can't meet our most important emotional needs ourselves—others must meet them for us.*

A marriage thrives when the spouses become experts at meeting each other's emotional needs. Being experts simply means that they have made an effort to learn what to do to make each other happy and they do it very well.

The wise couple will learn how to meet each other's emotional needs at expert level. Then, throughout their marriage, they will keep their skills finely tuned so that their relationship will be as fulfilling as possible for both spouses.

People take courses regularly to become experts at all sorts of things—typing, computer programming, hair styling, teaching. And at the beginning, learning any new skill may seem awkward and it usually requires some effort. Take typing, for example. At first it seems very unnatural. You search for every letter. But with practice typing becomes almost effortless and requires very little thought. You just know where the letters are because it has become a well-developed habit.

Habits that meet your spouse's needs develop in the same way. At first, they may seem uncomfortable to you but with practice they become a habit, part of who you are. A good marriage becomes almost effortless when spouses develop habits that meet each other's needs.

When Jon and Sue identified their five most important emotional needs, I asked them to make a trade. Jon would agree to become an expert in meeting Sue's most important emotional needs, and in return Sue would become an expert in meeting Jon's. But my problem with Sue and Jon was not in their *learning* how to meet each other's needs, it was in their *wanting* to meet each other's needs.

Sue did not want to meet Jon's need for sexual fulfillment. And Jon felt the same way about meeting Sue's need for affection and conversation. But if they didn't meet each other's emotional needs, the feeling of love they needed for their marriage would never materialize. Unless they met those needs for each other, there would not be enough love units deposited to trigger the feeling of love in either of them.

So I asked them to "prime the pump" to get love units flowing. Granted, it would have been much easier for them to meet each other's important emotional needs if they had been in love. But if they had waited for love before trying to meet each other's needs, they would still be waiting. My encouragement for both of them to make a trade and try to meet each other's emotional needs right away helped them start depositing those love units that were essential to their marital recovery.

> A good marriage becomes almost effortless when spouses develop habits that meet each other's needs.

Quality and Quantity

Jon knew how to meet Sue's emotional needs, but because he hadn't been doing it, he was a little rusty. To correct his mistakes and improve his overall performance, he needed feedback from Sue as to how well he was doing. He needed feedback on two aspects of his skill—quality and quantity.

To determine the quality of the way Jon was meeting Sue's needs, he was to ask, *Are you satisfied with the way I am meeting this need?*

If the answer was *no,* he would then ask, *How would you like me to meet this need?* Sue's response was to be specific and provide a positive suggestion. She was to avoid saying, *I don't like it when you do . . .* Instead, she was to say, *I would love it if you would do . . .* A positive suggestion is much more encouraging than a criticism.

To determine whether the quantity of need fulfillment was adequate, Jon was to ask Sue, *Do I meet this need for you often enough?*

> **A positive suggestion is much more encouraging than a criticism.**

If Sue's answer was *no*, then he was to ask, *How often would you like me to meet this need?* If she wanted more time talking with him or if she wanted him to show admiration for her more often or if she wanted more affection, he would then try to accommodate her wishes.

When you learn to meet each other's emotional needs, you will need to satisfy both the quality and quantity requirements to make your partner happy. Quantity is fairly easy to understand, because your partner will tell you how often and how much he or she wants the need met. But quality is more difficult to communicate. Sometimes even the one with the need doesn't understand exactly what's missing.

Not surprisingly Sue asked for more conversation, and that was very encouraging to Jon. It meant that she wanted him to deposit more love units, and the more he deposited, the closer he came to reaching her romantic love threshold. Sue didn't love him yet, but her willingness to let him meet her emotional needs meant that it was only a matter of time before they would be back to the terrific marriage they once had.

Meet Each Other's Needs in Ways That Are Mutually Enjoyable

When you ask each other to improve skills in need fulfillment, remember the four steps for negotiation that I discussed in chapter 7 (pages 99–103). The most important step is the first one, where you guarantee each other safety and a pleasant negotiating environment. If either of you becomes negative or unpleasant during your discussion, take a break and get back to your negotiations at a time when you can guarantee that the guidelines will be followed.

You should also remember to follow the Policy of Joint Agreement as you develop your new skills. It turns out that there will be many effective ways to meet each other's emotional needs. Some methods will be enjoyable for you to follow, and others may be very unpleasant. Because you are trying very hard to move toward marital recovery, you may be tempted to meet each other's needs at all costs. But I strongly advise you to avoid this.

> Never expect the other person to suffer or sacrifice so that your need can be met.

You should have an understanding that you will meet each other's needs only in ways that are enjoyable for both of you. Never expect the other person to suffer or sacrifice so that your need can be met. But since it is usually somewhat uncomfortable at first to form a new habit, make sure that you are not confusing the discomfort of learning something new with a behavior that will always be unpleasant to you. In other words, give a new habit a chance to become comfortable before you abandon it.

The topics of Sue and Jon's conversation had to be interesting to both of them. The recreational activities they chose had to be mutually enjoyable. They were willing to experiment with conversation and recreation. They tried different topics of conversation for a while and engaged in various recreational activities to see how they would feel about them.

But in the area of sexual fulfillment, they had a special problem. Before their separation, Sue had gotten into the habit of making love to Jon out of duty. Now that they were together again, she was still uncomfortable making love. Besides, being out of love with Jon made lovemaking particularly unappealing to her.

I suggested that they experiment with sex the same way they experimented with conversation and recreation. They had to try to find a way to make love that would satisfy Jon, yet still be comfortable for Sue.

Granted, at first, it was not exactly what Jon had in mind. He knew how passionate Sue could be, and their lovemaking certainly lacked passion as far as he was concerned.

But as Jon deposited more and more love units into Sue's Love Bank, he came closer and closer to triggering her love for him. It was only a matter of time before her feeling of love would be restored and, along with it, all the passion he had remembered.

Jon and Sue both knew how to meet each other's emotional needs. They had simply neglected to do it. But I've counseled many couples who have never learned how to meet certain needs. They must train themselves to become skilled in conversation or showing admiration or affection. If that's your situation and you must develop your ability to meet your spouse's important emotional needs, I refer you to my book, *His Needs, Her Needs: Building an Affair-proof Marriage.* In this book and its accompanying workbook, *Five Steps to Romantic Love,* I describe each of the most common needs of men and women and explain how to become an expert in meeting those needs.

You Can Be the Cause of Your Spouse's Greatest Happiness

You married each other because you were in love. And you were in love because you were meeting each other's most important emotional needs—you were the cause of each other's greatest happiness.

Since you have been married, you may have squandered your opportunity to be each other's source of greatest happiness. But it can be recovered by going back to what you did before you were married—making it your mission to meet each other's most important emotional needs.

> *You must be each other's greatest source of happiness if you want to have a successful marriage.*

You can be each other's greatest source of happiness. In fact you *must* be each other's greatest source of happiness if you want to have a successful marriage. You have given each other the opportunity to care in a way that no one else can care for you. And if you and your spouse don't use that opportunity, you will both feel that something important is missing.

You can be each other's greatest source of happiness if you become an expert at meeting each other's most important emotional needs. An important part of learning to be an expert is the respect you give to each other each step of the way.

First, you must identify each other's needs, and when you discover them you must be respectful regarding the needs themselves. It's tempting for all of us to be disrespectful of what we don't understand. When our spouse has needs that are different than ours, which is almost always the case, we may believe that the needs are unnecessary or even wrong. For example, the need for physical attractiveness is often viewed as superficial, reflecting a shallow attitude toward relationships. Those who believe this try to convince a spouse that he or she should learn not to have that need, or at least not to indulge it. The outcome, of course, it that the need is not met, and the spouse's opportunity to deposit love units is lost.

If you want to be the cause of your spouse's greatest happiness, you must begin by knowing what will create the greatest happiness for your spouse. Those turn out to be your spouse's most important emotional needs. Accept what you discover—an honest expression of your spouse's needs. If you don't, you will waste your time trying to meet needs that are of less importance to him or her.

> *Feedback from your spouse as to how you are doing at meeting his or her emotional needs is absolutely essential in your becoming an expert.*

After you identify each other's emotional needs, you must be respectful in the way you teach each other to become experts in meeting them. Feedback from your spouse as to how you are doing at meeting his or her emotional needs is absolutely essential in your becoming an expert. But if you want your spouse to be willing to give you feedback, you must receive it respectfully. A response that is defensive and even angry will end your spouse's willingness to help you become skilled. And respect is also necessary in the way feedback is expressed. Every time you discuss your skill development, Love Busters are in the wings ready to enter. And if you let them on stage, they will destroy the show. So remember to keep your conversation safe and pleasant whenever you discuss the way you meet each other's needs.

If you want to be the cause of each other's greatest happiness, you must identify each other's most important emotional needs, respectfully accept those needs, and use the Policy of Joint Agreement to develop skill in meeting those needs.

Sue and Jon could remember what it had been like to be the cause of each other's greatest happiness before the tragedy of the affair. But they didn't think they could completely recover from all of the resentment and hopelessness they were feeling. Deep down, they thought that their bad experiences would sentence them to a marriage that would never quite recover.

But they were wrong. They had new tools at their disposal that would not only help them recover the best feelings they had ever had for each other, but move them beyond that point. Their skills in meeting each other's needs would become unprecedented in their marriage. They still had a lot to learn but they were on their way toward creating a marriage that was more fulfilling than anything they could have ever imagined. They were on their way to becoming the cause of each other's greatest happiness.

Checklist for Following the Rule of Care:
Meet Your Spouse's Most Important Emotional Needs

Part 1: Identifying Your Most Important Emotional Needs

_____ Read appendix A to learn about the ten most important emotional needs.

_____ Make two enlarged copies of appendix B, the Emotional Needs Questionnaire, one for you and one for your spouse.

_____ Complete the questionnaire and rank your top five emotional needs according to their importance.

Part 2: Becoming an Expert at Meeting the Most Important Emotional Needs

_____ Agree to become an expert at meeting each other's top five emotional needs.

_____ Discover how to meet each other's emotional needs, regarding quantity and quality:

   _____ Ask your spouse, _How often would you like that need met?_

   _____ Ask your spouse, _How would you like me to meet your need?_

_____ Learn how to meet each other's emotional needs:

   _____ When giving feedback on quality, offer positive suggestions _(I'd love it if you would do . . .)_ instead of negative criticism.

   _____ Allow time for new behavior that meets emotional needs to first become comfortable and then become enjoyable.

   _____ Meet each other's needs in ways that are mutually enjoyable. Never expect your spouse to suffer.

   _____ Continue to give feedback to your spouse regarding your most important emotional needs.

   _____ Read _His Needs, Her Needs_ if you need help learning how to meet your spouse's important emotional needs.

MARITAL RECOVERY GUIDED BY
THE RULE OF TIME

Before Sue married Jon, she spent most of her free time with him. After they started dating, she made spending time with him one of her highest priorities. Whenever her friends invited her somewhere, she would first check with Jon to see if he was busy at that time. On some occasions she even broke dates with her friends if Jon found time to be with her.

Jon also made spending time with Sue his highest priority. Friends and activities that he had enjoyed prior to meeting Sue were abandoned because he had found a much more fulfilling relationship. He certainly didn't miss any of them, because he loved being with Sue.

Jon and Sue tried to see each other every day. When they were together, they usually gave each other their undivided attention. On days that they couldn't be together, they talked to each other on the phone, sometimes for hours. They spent about fifteen to twenty-five hours together each week, including time on the phone. But they weren't counting. Jon and Sue took whatever opportunities there were to be together, and it just turned out to be that much time.

After Jon and Sue were married, however, the quality of their time together suffered. While they were with each other more often, they spent less time giving each other their undivided attention. When they came home from work, they talked to each other as Sue prepared dinner and Jon helped pick things up around the apartment. They talked during dinner and they did the dishes together. But after dinner they watched television and sometimes barely said a word to each other. Some evenings Sue would read a book while Jon watched some sporting event. They usually went to bed at the same time and some evenings they made love. But even then they did not say much to each other.

Prior to marriage, when watching television, Jon and Sue would often be so affectionate that they didn't pay any attention to the program. But after marriage, they were rarely affectionate while watching TV. They usually sat in separate chairs, and sometimes watched in different rooms so that they could each see a favorite program.

Another important change after marriage was dating. Before marriage, Jon and Sue went out often—to dinner, a movie, sporting events, or they went for walks. Sue looked forward to being with Jon but she also looked forward to going out. She liked dating Jon, because they always did something fun together. After marriage they spent a lot of time just sitting at home watching TV.

When their children arrived, they went out even less often. And they talked to each other less. The children were a major distraction, and the responsibilities kept them both hopping. That was when Jon and Sue decided that he needed to put his career in high gear so that they could provide their children with a wonderful lifestyle. And that gave them even less time to be with each other.

Neither Jon nor Sue realized that after they married, their time together had ceased being a high priority. In fact almost everything else in their lives had become more important than their time together. Looking back, Jon and Sue could see how they had drifted apart. Jon was at work and away from his family—almost seventy hours each week. And when he was home, he was exhausted. Sue spent her days focused on her children, her work, and her community activities. Although she missed having Jon at home, she found her life too busy to worry much about it.

Now, even though Jon and Sue were committed to marital recovery, they found it difficult to schedule time to be together. They understood the importance of it, but actually scheduling their time turned out to be one of their most difficult assignments. They tried to talk me out of the amount of time I recommended. They began by trying to convince me that it's impossible. Then they went on to the argument that it's impractical. But in the end, Jon and Sue agreed that without a substantial amount of time together, they would not be able to meet each other's emotional needs and recreate the love they once had for each other. They agreed to follow my third rule to guide marital recovery, the Rule of Time: Take time to give your spouse your undivided attention.

The Rule of Time
Take time to give your spouse your undivided attention.

The purpose of the Rule of Time is to set aside enough time each week to meet your spouse's most important emotional needs. And meeting important emotional needs usually requires undivided attention. To help Jon and Sue fully understand the Rule of Time and how it was to be applied as they made their weekly schedules, I told them about the three parts to this rule: privacy, objectives, and amount.

Privacy: *The time you plan to be together should not include children, relatives, or friends. Establish privacy so that you are able to give each other your undivided attention.*

It is essential that you as a couple spend time alone. When you have time alone, you have a much greater opportunity to deposit love units into each other's Love Bank. Without privacy, undivided attention is almost impossible, and without undivided attention, you are not likely to meet some of each other's most important emotional needs.

First, I recommend that you learn to be together without your children. Many couples don't think children interfere with their privacy. To them, an evening with their children *is* privacy. Of course, they know they can't make love with children around. But I believe that the presence of children prevents much more than lovemaking. When children are present, they interfere with affection and intimate conversation that are desperately needed in marriage.

Second, I recommend that friends and relatives not be present during your time together. This may mean that after everything has been scheduled, there's no time left over for friends and relatives. If that's the case, you're too busy, but at least you won't be sacrificing your love for each other.

Third, I recommend that you understand what giving undivided attention means. Remember, it's what you did while dating. There's no way you would have been married if you had ignored each other on dates. You looked at each other when you were talking, you were interested in the conversation, and there was little to distract you. This is the undivided attention you must give each other now.

When you are seeing a movie together, you do not give each other undivided attention (unless you behave like one couple I remember who sat in front of my wife and me!). It's the same with television or sporting events. I'm not saying that you should not do these things together, but the time you spend at them doesn't count toward fulfilling the Rule of Time. That time is very clearly defined—it's the time you pay close attention to each other.

Jon and Sue recognized where they had gone wrong on the few dates they had with each other after being married. Jon would bring his cellular telephone along and become distracted by a business call while they were having dinner together. This left Sue feeling that she was low on his list of priorities. Whoever was on the other end of the telephone had to be much more important than she was.

Sue could also see how she had sabotaged their time together by inviting their children or another couple to join them at the last minute. Jon had wanted to be alone with Sue, but she usually insisted on including others on their night out. Now they both agreed to invite others on their dates *only after* they had spent enough time together by themselves.

Jon and Sue were committed to be alone with each other. But what should they do with this time? The second part of my Rule of Time deals with objectives.

Objectives: *During the time you are together, create activities that will meet the emotional needs of affection, sexual fulfillment, conversation, and recreational companionship.*

Time is valuable and should be used wisely. So when a couple schedules time for undivided attention, they should know precisely what they hope to accomplish with that time. Their goal should be to deposit as many love units as possible into each other's Love Bank. And the way to deposit the most love units is to meet each other's most important emotional needs.

Some important emotional needs can be met without undivided attention. For example, domestic support, family commitment, and financial support can be met without a spouse even being present. However, there are some emotional needs that can be met only with undivided attention. The most obvious one is sexual fulfillment. But affection, conversation, and recreational companionship are also best met in marriage with undivided attention.

For most men, sexual fulfillment and recreational companionship are among their top five emotional needs, and they are usually their top two. For most women, affection and conversation are their most important emotional needs. When all four come together, men and women alike call it romance and usually the combination deposits the most love units possible. My advice, then, is to try to combine them all when you schedule time for undivided attention.

After marriage some couples seem to lose the connection between these four emotional needs. Women may try to get their husbands to be affectionate and to talk to them without necessarily offering recreational companionship and sexual fulfillment in return. Men, on the other hand, may want their wives to meet their needs for recreational companionship and sexual fulfillment, without offering affection and conversation in return. Neither strategy works very well. Women usually resent having sex without affection and conversation first, and men usually resent being attentive and affectionate with no hope for sex and recreation. By combining the four needs into a single event, however, both spouses have their needs met and enjoy their time together.

If time is not set aside to meet all four needs, it is assumed that they can be met on the run—with no planning needed. A husband assumes that just because he is in bed with his wife at the end of a day, sex is there for the taking. His wife goes to bed dreading a possible ambush each night, while her husband fears rejection. A wife, on the other hand, assumes that her husband should drop whatever he's doing and be affectionate or talk with her whenever she feels the need. Not understanding that these four needs are best met when combined may make both spouses feel used and neglected.

The right way to meet all four emotional needs is to schedule enough time to meet them all. Trying to squeeze meeting these needs into an existing schedule is like buying shoes that are too small—the pain will be excruciating. You will simply not have enough time to do it right.

> *The right way to meet all four emotional needs is to schedule enough time to meet them all.*

When you schedule time for undivided attention, don't forget some of the other important emotional needs that can also be met during that time together, such as the need for physical attractiveness and admiration. When dating, you tried to present yourselves as attractively as possible to each other. You also tried to compliment each other whenever possible. Take a lesson from your courtship days and make sure that when you spend time together for undivided attention, you look your very best and express how much you value each other.

Keeping in mind the importance of meeting so many needs when you give each other your undivided attention, how much time should you schedule? That's what the third part of the Rule of Time helps us determine.

Amount: *The number of hours scheduled each week for undivided attention should reflect the quality of your marriage. If your marriage is satisfying to you and your spouse, schedule fifteen hours each week for your undivided attention. But if you suffer marital dissatisfaction, plan more time, until marital satisfaction is achieved.*

How much time do you need to sustain the feeling of romantic love? Believe it or not, there really is an answer to this question and it depends on the health of a marriage. If a couple is deeply in love with each other and find that their marital needs are being met, I have found that about fifteen hours each week of undivided attention is usually enough to sustain romantic love. It is probably the least amount of time necessary. If you are in love with each other and your emotional needs are being met by each other, you're either newly married or you have already been giving each other fifteen hours a week of your undivided attention.

When I apply the fifteen-hour principle to marriages, I usually recommend that the time be evenly distributed through the week, about two hours each day. When time must be bunched up—all hours on the weekend—good results are not as predictable. Spouses need to be emotionally connected on almost a daily basis to sustain their love for each other.

> *Spouses need to be emotionally connected on almost a daily basis to sustain their love for each other.*

The reason I have so much difficulty getting couples to spend time alone together is that when I first see them for counseling, they're not in love. Their relationship doesn't do anything for them, and the time spent with each other seems like a total waste at first. But when they spend time together, they learn to recreate the experiences that first met each other's emotional needs. And that time is spent redepositing love units into Love Bank accounts that are seriously overdrawn. Eventually, enough love units are deposited to trigger the feeling of love. That makes this time together much more appealing.

But without time to deposit love units, a couple have little hope of restoring the love they once had for each other. In fact for them, fifteen hours a week may not be enough. To jump-start their relationship may require twenty-five or thirty hours a week of undivided attention. This is why I usually recommend successive weekend trips, or a long vacation—this gives a couple time at the beginning of recovery to restore their love for each other.

When I mention trips and scheduling fifteen hours of time to give each other undivided attention, some couples find it unrealistic due to financial restrictions. But even those who have a limited budget can schedule time together, it just means being creative. Here are a few suggestions that might help.

- *Baby-sitting co-op.* One major roadblock for many is the cost of baby-sitting, added to the cost of going out. Child care is expensive these days. To help couples with this financial constraint, I have recommended joining or forming a baby-sitting co-op in your community or church. Another less formal idea is to simply ask friends with children if they would join in a weekly child swap—you watch their children one evening each week in exchange for their watching your children one evening.

- *Rearrange your budget priorities.* Many couples I have counseled have a comfortable lifestyle. Yet when it comes down to having money for weekend escapes together, they don't think they have enough. Jon and Sue were certainly in that category. They were in trouble financially but as they came to understand the importance of their time together, they were able to set aside enough money each month to go out a few evenings and occasionally to get away for weekends. The purpose of a budget is to be sure you have enough money available to achieve your life's objectives, and meeting important emotional needs in marriage should be your highest priority.

- *Be creative.* Meeting each other's important emotional needs doesn't have to be expensive. There are many ways you can get alone with each other to talk, be affectionate, be together recreationally, and make love without having to spend much money. Don't avoid going out together just because money is tight. Go out regularly but find things to do that you can afford.

Scheduling Time for Undivided Attention

Kevin and Lee, the couple we met in chapter 5, were off to a good start when it came to taking time for undivided attention. They began exercising together three times a week, having lunch together almost every day and talking on the phone several times during the day. They also scheduled Saturday night as their weekly date night. When they charted their time together, they consistently spent more than twenty hours each week with each other. Prior to Kevin's affair, they had given each other undivided attention less than an hour each week.

As soon as Kevin had recovered from the symptoms of withdrawal, his time with Lee met his emotional needs and deposited hundreds of love units in Lee's account. It wasn't long before he was in love with Lee again, and that made their time together even more enjoyable for him. Lee was also feeling more fulfilled than she had felt in years. Although Kevin's affair was an unwelcome trauma, she confessed to me that it shocked them out of their apathy. It forced them to create a new lifestyle that provided a fulfilling marriage.

Isn't it a shame that it took an affair to bring Kevin and Lee to their senses? Of course, Lee had not suffered anything close to what Jon suffered as a result of Sue's affair. But even Jon felt that her affair may have been necessary to bring him to a full understanding of how important it was to set aside time to meet Sue's emotional needs. And yet if Sue and Jon had not scheduled time to be alone with each other, even the lessons of the affair may have been all for nothing.

> A couple's love for each other cannot be created or sustained without time for undivided attention.

A couple's love for each other cannot be created or sustained without time for undivided attention. And unless you schedule time to meet each other's emotional needs, it won't get done. As I mentioned earlier, setting aside time to give each other undivided attention is one of the most difficult assignments I can give because the pressures of life usually crowd out the time it takes to sustain romantic love.

Jon and Sue brought their day planners to their session each week. We sat down and scheduled at least fifteen hours a week when they could give each other undivided attention. They decided what to do during those times and wrote it in. They also set aside a time at the end of each week to evaluate how well they did. Eventually they did the scheduling themselves. Jon and Sue got into a habit of every Sunday afternoon at 3:00 getting together and scheduling their time for the week to come.

> I recommend that you schedule the same hours week after week to be alone with your spouse.

Since we are creatures of habit, I recommend that you schedule the same hours week after week to be alone with your spouse. If you keep the same schedule every week, it will be easier to follow the Rule of Time.

The total amount of time you spend together doesn't necessarily affect the way you feel about each other in the week that the time is spent. It has more effect on the way you're going to feel about each other in future weeks. You are building your Love Bank accounts when you spend enjoyable time together, and the account must build before you feel the effect.

When Sue and Jon first started spending time together, their Love Bank accounts were in the red. It took several months for their accounts to rise to a level where they truly enjoyed each other's company. At first, they complained that their time together was uncomfortable and they had trouble finding things to talk about. But their efforts eventually paid off. They built their Love Bank accounts to a point where they brought out the very best in each other, and conversation became almost effortless.

You won't have to write your schedule of time together in your calendars for the rest of your life, although it will probably be something you won't mind doing after you get into the habit. For the first few weeks of recovery, however, write them in to help you get into some good habits. Then, once the habits are set and you are happy with the amount of time you spend with each other, you may not need to write the dates in your calendars anymore.

Make a bargain with each other that if either of you feels that your time together is deteriorating, you will get back to scheduling your dates on the calendar again. Take time to talk about how you have been spending your time together. This will help you see what's gone wrong. Discuss needed improvements in your behavior, and get into new habits that solve the problem.

Many couples mention that they see a noticeable improvement once they start scheduling time to be together. They also feel a noticeable irritability, resentment, and loneliness when time together is not set as a priority. Jon and Sue were very familiar with the hurtful feelings associated with their relationship having low priority. But in time, to avoid its recurrence, they got into the habit of scheduling their time for undivided attention.

Recreational Companionship

Jon and Sue discovered that they must do more than just schedule time to be together and give each other undivided attention. They had to make their time together the most enjoyable time of their week. But what should they do that they would both enjoy?

Many activities that they enjoyed in their twenties were no longer fun in their thirties. Or an activity that Jon still enjoyed was no longer enjoyable to Sue.

> Couples often make the fatal mistake of going their separate ways when an activity becomes boring to one of the spouses.

Couples often make the fatal mistake of going their separate ways when an activity becomes boring to one of the spouses. After all, they reason, why make one spouse sacrifice an enjoyable activity just to accommodate the other? If one spouse has become skilled playing golf, for example, why give it up just because the other spouse has lost interest in the sport?

The answers to those questions depend on the importance of love in your marriage. If the love you desire for each other is more important than your leisure activities, then you must spend your most enjoyable time with each other, and that time must be mutually enjoyable.

But if your leisure activities are more important than your love, then you should pursue your favorite activities independently of each other. If that's your choice, and if you don't spend your most enjoyable time together, you risk losing your emotional bond and your love for each other. If you choose to spend your most enjoyable leisure time apart, you not only miss an opportunity to build mutual love, but someone else may deposit enough love units into your Love Bank to risk an affair. Those are strong words, but as someone who has spent his life trying to save marriages, I know what I'm talking about.

Your love for each other should be more important to you than any leisure activity. That means that being with each other recreationally should be more important than the particular activity you choose to do together. The purpose of the activity should be to help build your relationship. It should not be the other way around. The purpose of your being together should not be to improve your skill in a particular recreational activity. You are not married because you enjoy playing tennis together. You play tennis together because it's a way of building your love for each other. If your spouse decides he or she doesn't enjoy tennis anymore, don't risk damaging your relationship by going off and playing tennis with someone else. Find an alternative to tennis that will be just as enjoyable for both of you.

It's extremely important to be each other's best friend throughout life. You do that by making each other a part of every enjoyable activity you have. If it's fun to do, your spouse should do it with you. If your spouse doesn't enjoy doing it, give it up. Whatever activity you choose—jogging, bicycling, playing football, golfing—be sure your spouse wants to do it too. Don't develop skills in an activity that your spouse does not enjoy.

One of the quickest ways to become bored with each other is to have more interesting things to do when you are apart. Eliminate that destructive possibility by deliberately spending your most enjoyable moments with each other. Spend as much of your leisure time together as possible and try to use that time to also meet the emotional needs of affection, conversation, and sexual fulfillment. Not only is spending leisure time together one of the best ways to build your relationship, but it ensures that the most interesting and enjoyable parts of your life are experienced together.

Checklist for Following the Rule of Time:
Take Time to Give Your Spouse Your Undivided Attention

Part 1: Privacy

_____ Schedule time to be together without children, relatives, or friends.

_____ Give each other your undivided attention.

Part 2: Objectives

_____ Create activities that will meet the emotional needs of affection, sexual fulfillment, conversation, and recreational companionship.

_____ Choose recreational activities that will build your marital relationship as your primary objective.

_____ Choose recreational activities that are mutually enjoyable.

Part 3: Amount

_____ Schedule in advance of each week at least fifteen hours for undivided attention.

_____ Overcome financial obstacles that prevent giving each other undivided attention:

     _____ Join or start a baby-sitting co-op.

     _____ Rearrange your budget priorities.

     _____ Be creative and choose inexpensive recreational activities.

_____ Choose a time each week to schedule your dates for the next week.

Marital Recovery Guided by
The Rule of Honesty

Sue broke all the rules when she had an affair with Greg. She broke the Rule of Protection because she knew her relationship with Greg would be devastating to Jon but she did it anyway. She broke the Rule of Care after her affair began because she stopped meeting Jon's important emotional needs. She broke the Rule of Time because she avoided spending time with him. In fact she finally left him so that she would not need to spend any time with him at all.

But the rule she broke that may have done her marriage the most harm was the Rule of Honesty. Throughout her marriage to Jon, Sue valued their mutual honesty. But when her affair began, honesty was abandoned, and dishonesty was shifted into high gear. It was her pervasive dishonesty that turned her love for Greg into a marital disaster.

Kevin took a different path. When he knew he was in love with Amy, he thought about lying to Lee about it, but it didn't take him long to reject that option. By honestly expressing his feelings to his wife, he avoided the year of agony that Sue and Jon had to bear. If Sue had taken the path of honesty, she too could have avoided most of the misery that she imposed on herself and her family.

Radical honesty is essential for marital recovery after an affair. Honesty not only points a couple toward their goal of reconciliation, but it also helps restore trust. Of course, as is the case with each of the four rules of marriage, honesty is essential to creating a great marriage—period. But almost all affairs *require* dishonesty. An honest relationship between a husband and wife makes affairs almost impossible. So if a couple has any hope of recovering trust after an affair, they must create a level of honesty never before achieved in their marriage.

To help couples understand the importance of honesty, I've created the Rule of Honesty: Be totally open and honest with your spouse.

The Rule of Honesty
Be totally open and honest with your spouse.

When you follow this rule, you should reveal to your spouse as much information about yourself as you know—your thoughts, feelings, habits, likes, dislikes, personal history, daily activities, and plans for the future.

You may agree with me that spouses should be honest with each other but you may wonder how far honesty should go. To help couples understand this rule, I have broken it down into its five parts:

1. *Emotional honesty:* Reveal your emotional reactions—both positive and negative—to the events of your life, particularly to your spouse's behavior.
2. *Historical honesty:* Reveal information about your personal history, particularly events that demonstrate personal weakness or failure.
3. *Current honesty:* Reveal information about the events of your day. Provide your spouse with a calendar of your activities, with special emphasis on those that may affect your spouse.
4. *Future honesty:* Reveal your thoughts and plans regarding future activities and objectives.
5. *Complete honesty:* Do not leave your spouse with a false impression about your thoughts, feelings, habits, likes, dislikes, personal history, daily activities, or plans for the future. Do not deliberately keep personal information from your spouse.

To some extent this rule seems like motherhood and apple pie. Who would argue that it's *not* a good idea to be honest? But in my years of experience as a marriage counselor, I have found that many clients consider dishonesty a good idea under certain circumstances.

Granted, dishonesty may seem like a good short-term solution to marital conflict. It'll probably get you off the hook for a few days or months. But it's a terrible long-term solution. If you expect to build a relationship of trust that will last throughout your life, total honesty is essential.

To those who argue that dishonesty can be justified under certain circumstances, I must say that my Rule of Honesty leaves no room for exceptions. But because there are so many out there who advocate dishonesty in marriage, I need to build a case for my position. Let's take a careful look at each of the five parts of this rule, beginning with emotional honesty.

Emotional Honesty

Sue found it very difficult to express her emotional reactions, particularly the negative ones. She was afraid that Jon would judge her and she certainly did not want Jon to be hurt by those feelings. She did not feel capable of expressing negative feelings without anger, disrespect, or demands. So she didn't express them at all.

> ### Emotional Honesty
> *Reveal your emotional reactions—both positive and negative—to the events of your life, particularly to your spouse's behavior.*

Sue also felt that any negative reactions would reflect the fact that she did not accept Jon unconditionally. She wanted unconditional acceptance from him and she thought that her own negative reactions would encourage him to be critical of her.

But negative feelings serve a valuable purpose in marriage. They are a signal that something is wrong. If Sue had learned to steer clear of angry outbursts, disrespectful judgments, and selfish demands, her honest expression of negative feelings would have alerted Jon to an adjustment that would have made their marriage much more enjoyable.

Honesty enables couples to make appropriate adjustments to each other, and adjustment is what a good marriage is all about. Jon and Sue needed to adjust to each other as their surroundings and their needs changed. But how could they adjust without accurate information from each other? That's flying blind—like a pilot whose instrument panel has shorted out.

To adjust successfully, you need a steady flow of accurate data from each other. Without this, unhappy situations can go on and on. But if you communicate your feelings to each other, you can correct what you're doing wrong before it withdraws too many love units.

The mere communication of feelings does not assure that all the necessary adjustments will be made. There is still work to do. But without that honest communication, failure is guaranteed.

The expression of negative reactions is important, but don't overlook the expression of positive feelings. While positive feelings are generally easier to communicate than negative ones, many couples have not learned to express these feelings either. Failing to do so, they miss an important opportunity to deposit love units. If you say clearly and enthusiastically that you like something your spouse has done, you'll make your partner feel good, knowing that his or her care is appreciated.

Historical Honesty

Should your skeletons stay in the closet?

Some say, *Yes. Lock the door; hide the key; leave well enough alone. Communicate your past misdeeds only on a need-to-know basis.*

But I say your spouse needs to know everything. Whatever embarrassing experiences or serious mistakes are in your past, you need to come clean with him or her.

Your personal history holds significant information about you—information about your strengths and weaknesses. Your spouse needs to fully understand both your good and bad characteristics. Under what conditions are you the most caring and considerate? Where are you likely to be most self-centered and hurtful?

History tends to repeat itself. For example, if a man has had problems controlling his temper in the past, it's likely he'll have the same struggle in the future. If a woman has been chemically dependent in the past, she'll be susceptible to drug or alcohol abuse in the future. If you talk openly about your past mistakes, your spouse will understand your weaknesses, and together you can avoid situations that will tend to create problems for you in the future.

Historical Honesty

Reveal information about your personal history, particularly events that demonstrate personal weakness or failure.

No area of your life should be kept secret. All questions asked by your spouse should be answered fully and completely. Periods of poor adjustment in your past should be given special attention. Be sure that both you and your spouse understand what happened in those previous circumstances. That way you will be able to create a lifestyle together that does not tempt your weaknesses.

Not only should *you* explain your past to your spouse, but you should encourage your spouse to gather information from those who knew you before. I have encouraged couples who are considering marriage to meet with several significant people from each other's past. It's often quite an eye-opener!

But if I tell her about all the bad things I've done, she'll never trust me again.

If he finds out about my past, he'll be crushed. It will ruin his whole image of me.

I have heard these protests from various clients—ashamed of things they had done. *Why dig it all up? Let old mistakes stay buried in ancient history! Why not just leave that little demon alone?* I answer that it's not a "little demon," but an extremely important part of their personal story and it says something about their character.

Maybe you don't really want to be known for who you are. That's the saddest position of all. It means you would rather keep your secret than experience one of life's greatest joys—to be loved and accepted in spite of known weaknesses or past mistakes.

As Sue and Jon learned to be honest with each other, they began to reveal some of the significant events of their past that they had kept secret. When they first came to me for counseling, I had them complete a personal history questionnaire, which systematically reviewed many of the significant events of their past. I asked them to share their questionnaires with each other and feel free to ask any questions that would be triggered by them.

To help you and your spouse investigate each other's past, I have provided a copy of my Personal History Questionnaire in appendix C. Make two enlarged copies of it, one for each of you, and complete them as honestly as you can. Leave nothing out and be willing to pursue any line of inquiry that will help you understand each other better.

Current Honesty

After eight years of marriage, Sue found herself in love with another man. She did not develop her friendship with Greg because she wanted to have an affair. Quite to the contrary, she didn't want an affair at all. But once she was in love with Greg, an affair seemed inevitable. She did nothing to stop it, and her dishonesty made it all possible.

> ### Current Honesty
> *Reveal information about the events of your day. Provide your spouse with a calendar of your activities, with special emphasis on those that may affect your spouse.*

Sue spent an increasing amount of time with Greg because she loved him. But to keep Jon in the dark, she had to lie about the time they spent together. It was only after he found them making love that Jon realized that she had been living a secret second life. Dishonesty became a habit for her.

Kevin, on the other hand, had been in the habit of revealing his daily schedule to Lee. If he had decided to pursue his affair with Amy, he would have had to *learn* to be dishonest about how he spent his time. That's one of the reasons he told Lee about his affair as soon as it started and why it was possible for him to end it quickly—

because he was not in the habit of being dishonest. Current honesty made it easier for Kevin to end his affair than for Sue to end hers.

In good marriages couples become so interdependent that sharing a daily schedule is essential to their coordination of activities. In weak marriages, however, couples are reluctant to reveal their schedules, because they are often engaged in activities that would offend each other. Assuming that their spouse would object to these activities, they hide the details of their day, telling themselves, *What he doesn't know won't hurt him* or *She's happier not knowing everything*.

Even when activities are innocent, it's extremely important for your spouse to understand what you do with your time, because almost everything you do will affect your spouse in some way. Make sure you are easy to find in an emergency or when your spouse just wants to say hello during the day.

Future Honesty

Kevin's honesty about his future plans was crucial to his success in ending the affair. He was in love with Amy, and they planned to deepen their relationship. By revealing those plans to Lee, he took the first step toward saving his marriage. Because he considered Lee's feelings before he made further plans with Amy, those plans were eliminated.

Sue, on the other hand, had not been in the habit of revealing her plans to Jon before her affair. That's part of the reason the affair was so difficult to end. But even as they were trying to restore their marriage after the affair, she had trouble being honest about her plans. She was in the habit of making her plans independently of Jon, and bringing him into those plans felt very uncomfortable. By including him in her planning process, she thought he would have too much influence over her. She wanted to think her plans through on her own, and then, maybe, she would share her final decisions with him.

After I've made such a big issue of revealing past indiscretions, you can imagine how I feel about revealing future plans that may get you into trouble. Future plans are much easier to discuss than past mistakes or failures, yet, like Sue, many spouses keep their plans secret from each other. Why? Some people believe that communicating future plans just gives a spouse the opportunity to stop them.

They have their sights set on a certain goal and they don't want anything to stand in their way.

Future Honesty

Reveal your thoughts and plans regarding future activities and objectives.

When you fail to tell your spouse about your plans, you're not being honest. You may be trying to avoid trouble in the present, but eventually the future will arrive, revealing your thoughtless plans. At that point your spouse will be hurt that you didn't take his or her feelings into account when you were making those plans. And that will certainly withdraw love units.

The Policy of Joint Agreement—*Never do anything without an enthusiastic agreement between you and your spouse*—is crucial in discussions of your future plans. But spouses are often afraid to discuss those plans with the Policy of Joint Agreement in mind. *If I wait for my wife to agree,* a husband might say, *we'll never accomplish anything. She's so conservative; she never wants to take any risks, and so we miss every opportunity that comes along.* But isn't that a disrespectful judgment, forcing the husband's opinion on the wife? If her feelings are important to him, he needs her input on his plans. Without it, he risks gaining at her expense.

Oh, but the plans I make are best for both of us, a wife might say. *He may not understand my decision now but once he sees how things turn out, he'll thank me for going ahead with it.* Again, her plan of action is disrespectful. It assumes the husband's judgment is so poor that his wife must make his decisions for him. She would not want him to be that disrespectful of her judgments, and yet her example may very well lead to that outcome.

Whatever your reason for keeping your spouse in the dark about your plans, your decision will eventually give you more trouble than it's worth. And when it's discovered, love units will certainly be withdrawn.

Information about gifts or plans for special occasions may be the rare exception to the rule of future honesty. But in the recovery of your relationship after an affair, I would not be dishonest even under these special conditions until your marriage is completely restored.

When you plan to give each other gifts, you should explain your plans and then follow the Policy of Joint Agreement (Ask, *How do you feel about what I am planning to give you?*). Honesty in your marriage is so important right now that you cannot afford to keep secrets from each other even when they may seem harmless.

Complete Honesty

I ask probing questions when I counsel. And I probe most deeply in areas where people tend to leave false impressions. Since most marital problems originate with serious misconceptions, I do what I can to dig out these little weeds that eventually choke the plant. It goes without saying that false impressions are just as deceitful as outright lies.

The purpose of honesty is having the facts in front of you. Without them, you'll fail to solve the simplest marital problems. Lying to your spouse or giving false impressions will leave your spouse ignorant of the facts.

Complete Honesty

Do not leave your spouse with a false impression about your thoughts, feelings, habits, likes, dislikes, personal history, daily activities, or plans for the future. Do not deliberately keep personal information from your spouse.

In most marriages one of the biggest false impressions may be that both spouses are doing an outstanding job meeting each other's needs. This form of deceit is often tempting early in marriage. There may have been some areas in which one or both of you were dissatisfied, but you didn't want to appear unappreciative. You didn't want to run the risk of withdrawing love units by expressing your dissatisfaction.

As I mentioned earlier, you can minimize the loss of love units by expressing your concerns in nonthreatening, nonjudgmental ways. You can show appreciation for the effort made to meet your needs and then provide an alternative behavior that provides guidance for making that effort more effective. But only a true expression of your feelings will help you find a solution to your problems. Whenever you do not reveal the compete truth, you cripple your spouse's ability to meet your needs. You provide a map that leads to failure. Truth is the only map that leads to success.

Creating an Environment for Honesty

Sue needed to learn to be honest with Jon. But Jon needed to learn how to create an environment where her honesty would be encouraged. I wanted him to reward her for her honesty. In the past he had done the opposite.

Finally presented with the truth about something that had been concealed, many spouses think only of punishment. They cry; they scream; they hit; they threaten—and all these things just convince the lying partner to cover his or her crimes more carefully in the future.

Don't make your spouse miserable when he or she tells you the truth. That simply encourages dishonesty the next time. Instead, talk about how important honesty is to you and how you want to work together to achieve greater love and compatibility. Use the disclosure as evidence that you both need to rise to a new level of honesty.

How well do you encourage honesty? You may say that you want your spouse to be honest, but do your own values promote it? How do you answer the following questions?

1. If the truth is terribly upsetting to you, do you want your spouse to be honest only at a time when you are emotionally prepared?
2. Do you keep some aspects of your life secret and do you encourage your spouse to respect your privacy or boundaries in those areas?
3. Do you like to create a certain mystery between you and your spouse?
4. Are there conditions under which you would not want honesty at all costs between you and your spouse?

If you answer *yes* to any of these questions, you do not always value honesty. In certain situations, you feel your marriage is better off with dishonesty. You see, there are always "reasons" to be dishonest. But that little crack is all dishonesty needs to slip into your marriage and run amok. As soon as you allow one reason for dishonesty, it becomes easier to allow others, and before you know it, you have a dishonest relationship.

You encourage honesty when you *value* honesty. If your own values do not consistently support honesty, you will be sending each other mixed messages that will undermine the Rule of Honesty.

You encourage honesty when you value honesty.

Having consistent values is one way to encourage honesty. But another important way to encourage it is in the way you react to honesty. Do your reactions convey an appreciation for the truth, even if it's painful? These questions will help you determine if you are actually discouraging honesty in the way you sometimes react to it.

1. Do you ever have angry outbursts when your spouse is honest with you?
2. Do you ever make disrespectful judgments when your spouse is honest with you?
3. Do you ever make selfish demands when your spouse is honest with you?

If you answered *yes* to any of these questions, you are using Love Busters to punish honesty and you are inadvertently encouraging dishonesty. The way to encourage each other to be truthful is to minimize the negative consequences of truthful revelations. Instead of trying to punish your spouse when a shocking truth is revealed, try to reward your spouse's honesty.

I have had couples learn to say, *Thank you for being honest.* If they feel they need some time to process the new information, so as to protect their spouse from any Love Buster, I have them add, *Can I have ten minutes to think about this and then we'll get back together to talk about it?*

There are some marriages so infected by the Love Buster angry outbursts that it is not safe to be honest. Honesty runs the risk of a severe beating or even death. In these marriages, I suggest that a couple separate until safety can be assured. No couple should live together as long as one spouse persists in abusing the other. And if honesty triggers physical or emotional abuse, separation is usually the only reasonable response. Dishonesty may prevent physical and emotional abuse in the short run but dishonesty can lead to even greater abuse when it is discovered. If the fear of abuse is preventing you from being honest, I suggest separation while the abusive spouse receives professional treatment. Then when the risk of abuse is overcome, be totally honest with your spouse.

Remember, honesty is never your enemy; it's a friend that brings light to a problem that often needs a creative solution. If honesty is followed by safe and pleasant negotiation, it becomes the necessary first step toward improving your compatibility and love for each other.

Don't Wrap Your Honesty in Love Busters

Not only can a spouse's reaction to honesty be a Love Buster, but the honest revelation can actually be a Love Buster in disguise.

What if you were to express your unhappiness by throwing a lamp and crying out, *You never have time for me anymore. I don't know why I ever married you, you selfish jerk.* You might get points for honesty but they'd all be lost because of your angry outburst. It does no good to express genuine feelings if your spouse is running for cover.

Instead of getting angry, you might say, *I'm the least important person in your life. Your priorities are certainly screwed up. You seem to think that money is more important than I am.* That may be your honest opinion, but you are wrapping it in a disrespectful judgment—you are telling your spouse how he or she feels. The truth is that you don't know how your spouse feels, unless he or she tells you.

Or you might say, *If you don't start spending more time with me soon, I'll find someone else to spend time with and you'll be sleeping with your money.* That's a selfish demand. It's an ultimatum with a threat of punishment if the demand is not met.

There are better ways to express your honesty. For example, *I become upset when I'm left alone at night. I'd love to spend more time with you. Can we talk about ways to make this happen?* These are honest statements of your feelings, because you are telling your spouse how you feel and what you would like and you are suggesting the creation of a plan to see that it happens.

Sometimes it feels awkward to avoid angry outbursts, disrespectful judgments, and selfish demands. If you are in the habit of using these Love Busters to try to get your way, they may seem to be a part of your normal conversation. But anyone can learn to avoid them if a concerted effort is made to drive them out completely. And once they are no longer a part of your conversation, the chances that your spouse will listen to you and grant your requests are greatly increased.

> If you are to be honest with your spouse, you must be willing to reveal your feelings without Love Busters.

If you are to be honest with your spouse, you must be willing to reveal your feelings but you must reveal them without Love Busters. That way honesty will help your marriage instead of hurting it.

Honesty Means Being Persistent

It is not true that Sue never told Jon how she felt. She occasionally said, *I'm lonely.* But Jon would say, *Well, I don't know how we can pay the bills if I'm home all the time.* Sue eventually stopped saying it but she continued to feel lonely. She just learned to live with it. Jon thought it was no longer a problem because Sue stopped talking about it.

Communication cannot happen unless two people are both expressing and receiving honest feelings, hearing and honoring complaints, and understanding and accepting important data. But it will often be the case that your complaints are not heard or the data you convey is not received. Then persistence is important. Your commitment to honesty does not end when you have reported a feeling. You must continue to express your feelings honestly until the problem is resolved. In other words, Sue should have confronted Jon on a regular basis because she was feeling lonely on a regular basis.

Sue's repeated request for a resolution to her problem may seem like nagging, but there is a difference between repeating your negative emotional reactions and nagging. The difference is Love Busters. Nagging adds angry outbursts, disrespect, and demands to your honest expression. Expressing negative emotional reactions without Love Busters is fulfilling your commitment to honesty. When you tell your spouse that a problem has not yet been solved and the two of you need to keep thinking of solutions, you are being honest. I encourage you to repeat that expression of dissatisfaction until your problem is solved. But do it in a cheerful and nonthreatening way.

Remember, honesty is essential for a successful marriage. Persistently sharing your honest feelings until a problem is solved is also essential. This combination gives a couple opportunities to make appropriate adjustments to each other that lead to mutual happiness.

Checklist for Following the Rule of Honesty:
Be Totally Open and Honest with Your Spouse

_____ Reveal your emotional reactions—both positive and negative—to the events of your life, particularly to your spouse's behavior (emotional honesty).

_____ Reveal information about your personal history, particularly events that demonstrate personal weakness or failure (historical honesty).

_____ Complete the Personal History Questionnaire in appendix C to learn more about each other's personal history.

_____ Reveal information about the events of your day. Provide your spouse with a calendar of your activities, with special emphasis on those that may affect your spouse (current honesty).

_____ Reveal your thoughts and plans regarding future activities and objectives (future honesty).

_____ Do not leave your spouse with a false impression about your thoughts, feelings, habits, likes, dislikes, personal history, daily activities, or plans for the future. Do not deliberately keep personal information from your spouse (complete honesty).

_____ Create an environment that encourages honesty by valuing total honesty.

_____ Create an environment that encourages honesty by avoiding angry outbursts, disrespect, and demands when your spouse is being honest with you.

_____ Avoid angry outbursts, disrespect, and demands when you are being honest with your spouse.

_____ Be persistently honest if a situation that is bothering you doesn't improve.

_____ If there is a threat of abuse from your spouse when you express your honest feelings, separate from your spouse until he or she can guarantee your protection when you are being honest.

Managing Resentment and Restoring Trust

Completing Marital Recovery Part 1

Jon felt betrayed, deceived, abandoned, and very angry when he discovered Sue's affair. After all, it was hatched with full knowledge of the pain it would inflict on him. It reflected a total disregard for Jon's feelings, someone whom Sue had promised to cherish and protect for life.

At first, Jon could not imagine ever having a normal relationship with Sue again. The image of Sue in bed with Greg was not only sickening to him, but also infuriating. Resentment greatly understates what he actually felt whenever that memory came to his mind.

When Sue left him, she told him that she needed time to "sort out" her feelings. Jon knew what that meant—whoever made her feel the best, he or Greg, would win the prize of having her as a wife. The resentment that Jon felt seemed unbearable.

But there was more. After going back and forth a few times, trying to "get in touch" with her feelings, Sue tossed Jon out of his own home, separating him from his own children. And then, when the affair finally ended and Sue was rejected by her lover, she asked Jon to return. It wasn't Sue's choice; it was her lover's choice. Jon won by default. Resentment doesn't begin to describe Jon's angry reaction.

But remarkably, the resentment that a betrayed spouse feels does not usually lead to divorce. In fact most betrayed spouses, like Jon, are willing to reconcile in spite of their resentment. However, when these couples try to reconcile, resentment and the fear of a new affair often threaten the ultimate success of the recovery.

Resentment is a normal reaction to someone who has made you suffer. It is the way your emotions have of warning you to avoid people who have hurt you in the past—they may hurt you again in the future! But resentment can also be an irrational reaction to something that is no longer a real threat. Resentment itself may become a greater obstacle to your happiness than what it is you resent.

Most couples I have counseled know how damaging their feelings of resentment are to their happiness and to the future of their marriage. But some seem unable to stop it. It's an interesting subject for a psychologist who is supposed to know how to help people control their thoughts and emotions. But, I must admit, this is a tough reaction to control, especially when memories are so painful.

Living with the Memory of an Affair

When a couple tries to reconcile after an affair, they may try to forgive and forget. But while all may be forgiven, all is not forgotten. It is impossible to forget a spouse's unfaithfulness, unless all memory goes along with it.

But one of the most remarkable discoveries of my career as a marriage counselor is that in spite of the memory of an affair, marriages can thrive.

Before infidelity actually happens, most couples think they could not continue in a marriage after an affair. The memories would be too painful. But what people think they will do with a wayward spouse isn't what they usually do.

Surprisingly enough, after the dust settles, most couples I've counseled try to reconcile. Even though the memory can't be erased, they can survive the affair and create a thriving marriage. But what do they do with the resentment they feel as they try to reconcile?

The More There Is to Resent, the More Difficult Resentment Is to Overcome

Betrayed spouses almost always feel resentment. Both Jon and Lee were resentful about their spouse's affair. But Kevin's decisiveness in ending his affair early gave Lee much less to resent, and her resentment was easier to overcome. Sue's vacillation between Greg and Jon, and then her eventual separation from Jon, greatly increased Jon's suffering and his reasons to be resentful.

When it became apparent that Sue's affair would not end as quickly as most, I encouraged Jon to avoid seeing or talking to her until her affair was over (my plan B). The reason I encouraged him to avoid Sue while her affair was going on was to minimize his resentment. By avoiding Sue entirely, he had fewer memories of her affair when she was finally ready to reconcile. Although this step helped to minimize Jon's painful experiences, Sue's irresponsible behavior still made his resentment both overwhelming and inevitable.

> *An emotional reaction to a painful event fades over time, as long as that painful event is not repeated.*

An emotional reaction to a painful event fades over time, as long as that painful event is not repeated. But the more it is repeated, the more firmly fixed the memory becomes. In Jon's case, the painful events of Sue's affair were repeated again and again, and with each blow, his resentment was intensified.

I offered Jon and Sue a plan for reconciliation after the affair, but I knew the plan wouldn't work if Jon wasn't able to handle his feelings of resentment that were certain to accompany his reconciliation with Sue. If feelings of resentment are not dealt with correctly, they can ruin an otherwise stunning recovery.

Focusing on the Present and Future Can Help Diminish Resentment

As I've already said, we can never completely forget a spouse's betrayal, but we can make an effort not to dwell on that painful event. As we spend less and less time thinking about the betrayal, the memory of it will fade, along with the resentment we feel.

One of the reasons I'm not so keen on dredging up the past as a part of therapy is that it brings up memories that carry resentment along with them. If I'm not careful, a single counseling session can open up such a can of worms that the presenting problem gets lost in the flood of painful memories. If the goal of therapy is to "resolve" every past issue, that seems to me to be a good way to keep people coming to therapy for the rest of their lives. I believe that resolving issues of the past is an insurmountable goal. We simply cannot learn to feel good about something that caused us pain.

Instead, as a therapist, I tend to focus my attention on the present and the future, because we can do something about them. The past is impossible to change. Why waste our effort on things we have no control over, when we can put that same effort into plans that will bring us a fulfilling future? Granted, it's useful to learn lessons from the past, but we must learn the lessons and then move on.

I believe this focus on the future is the way to deal with feelings of resentment. Let me illustrate this through Jon's experience. When Jon expressed to me his resentment about the way Sue had treated him, I told him that we would put the issue of his resentment on hold as we focused on ways he and Sue could avoid making the same mistakes in the future. I asked him to trust my judgment and wait to see what happened to his resentment after his marriage had a chance to recover. Only on rare occasions do I need to help a betrayed spouse overcome resentment after marital recovery. I've found that when marriages recover completely, using my four rules, resentment almost always fades away. And that's what happened to Jon. By postponing discussions about resentment, we put off an issue that took care of itself.

When the four rules to guide marital recovery are followed, the couple avoid Love Busters, they meet each other's emotional needs, they spend time together, and they are honest with each other. That will eliminate the root causes of infidelity. But if the four rules are not followed, recovery will not be complete—needs will not be met and Love Busters will persist. Then resentment is created in the present, which triggers resentment of the past.

> When marriages recover completely, using my four rules, resentment almost always fades away.

Avoid Using Resentment as a Love Buster

Resentment and Love Busters have a great deal in common. Love Busters, particularly angry outbursts, disrespectful judgments, and selfish demands, are ways we may be tempted to react once we feel resentful. In other words, resentment is a feeling, and Love Busters are tempting reactions to that feeling.

There are many who react to their feeling of resentment by inflicting punishment on their spouse for past sins. They express their "feeling" as an angry outburst. But it is pure and simple abuse, disguised as the expression of honest feelings. No spouse has the right to punish the other spouse, and when resentment is felt, an angry outburst must be avoided at all costs.

> Resentment is a feeling, and Love Busters are tempting reactions to that feeling.

Some react to resentment by making demands on their spouse. Sadly the tactic often works. The spouse will give in to the demand because he or she feels guilty about having had the affair. It's a Love Buster because it makes the spouse who must meet the demand very unhappy.

I received a letter from a woman who had had an affair ten years earlier. She said that whenever she and her husband had an argument or she was reluctant to have sex, he would bring up the fact that she had an affair. Being reminded of her affair would throw her off balance emotionally and make her feel guilty. To avoid his anger, and soothe her guilty feelings, she usually gave in to his demands.

I advised the woman to look her husband right in the eye and say to him, *Listen Buster, do you love me? Do you want me to love you? Do you want to spend the rest of your life with me? If the answer to any of those questions is yes, you sure are going about it the wrong way. I will not give you what you want when you try to make me feel guilty. If you want to make love to me more often, let's negotiate. But what I did is in the past. Please do not bring it up any more. I will not let you treat me this way because it will ruin my love for you.*

My advice to her husband is to avoid mentioning the affair again. When you keep bringing up your spouse's past mistakes, not only do you make your conversation incredibly unpleasant, but it cannot possibly lead to a resolution of a conflict that you may be discussing.

Sometimes when a person can't seem to let go of an unpleasant thought, it is because that thought is somehow helpful to him or her. Even though the thought is unpleasant, it gets the person something. The letter writer's husband is a good example of this technique. The thought of his wife's affair was unpleasant but it was useful—bringing it up got him what he wanted. If the wife makes sure her husband never gets what he wants when he brings up the affair, he will eventually let go of his resentment because it is no longer useful to him.

Jon was very tempted to use Love Busters in response to his feelings of resentment. But he understood how important it was for him to restore Sue's feelings of love for him and he knew that Love Busters would make her hate him, not love him. So he resisted angry outbursts, disrespectful judgments, and selfish demands, even when his feelings of resentment seemed overwhelming.

Restoring Trust

An emotional reaction closely related to resentment is the loss of trust. After an affair, a betrayed spouse not only feels resentful about the way he or she was hurt by the wayward spouse, but the betrayed spouse also feels that he or she can never trust that wayward spouse again. And without trust, how can a marriage ever be fulfilling?

> Trust is the belief that our spouse will be honest with us and will protect our feelings.

Trust is the belief that our spouse will be honest with us and will protect our feelings. In other words, trust assumes that our spouse will follow the Rule of Honesty and the Rule of Protection. Before Sue's affair, Jon had trusted her to be honest with him and to avoid doing anything that would hurt him. More to the point, he had trusted Sue to avoid having an affair. But she had proven to be dishonest. She had looked right into Jon's eyes and lied to him. Then, faced with undeniable evidence, she had grudgingly and defensively admitted to one lie after another, but it was rarely accompanied by an apology. Considering her obvious failure to be honest and protect Jon's feelings, could he ever trust her again?

One reason I had Jon and Sue learn to follow the Rule of Honesty and the Rule of Protection was so they could restore their trust in each other. Those two rules encapsulated the meaning of trust, and by learning to follow those rules, they would learn to trust each other again.

I have counseled many spouses who refuse to follow the Rule of Protection. In other words, they admit that they are willing to let their spouse suffer so they can get what they want. When the spouse of an alcoholic complains that drinking causes unhappiness, he or she drinks anyway. Workaholics do the same thing. Their spouse's feelings have little effect on their decisions. They do what they want, regardless of the negative effect on their spouse.

Whenever someone's spouse is unwilling to follow the Rule of Protection, I explain to that person that their spouse should not be trusted. Why? Because we trust those who are willing and able to protect our feelings, and someone unwilling to follow the Rule of Protection is unwilling to protect our feelings. That person may have never had an affair, may not be an alcoholic, a workaholic, or any other kind of "aholic." That person may have never done anything to upset his or her spouse, but the unwillingness to follow the Rule of Protection means that it's only a matter of time before thoughtlessness rears its ugly head.

Sue and Jon had never understood trust that way before. They had always thought of trust as something you simply did when you were married. You had to trust your spouse. But I explained that trust grows as each spouse shows himself or herself to be trustworthy. Unless both of them were willing to follow the Rule of Honesty and Rule of Protection, they should not trust each other. On the other hand, as soon as they both followed those rules, they could trust each other immediately.

Of course, trust cannot be turned on and off like a light switch, and they both had to prove that they were trustworthy. By following the Rule of Honesty and Rule of Protection they would eventually prove their trustworthiness to each other.

> Someone unwilling to follow the Rule of Protection is unwilling to protect our feelings.

If someone who has a long history of dishonesty and thoughtlessness agrees to the Rule of Honesty and the Rule of Protection, that person is on his or her way to becoming trustworthy, in spite of past history. As he or she learns how to be honest and learns how to follow the Policy of Joint Agreement (the essence of the Rule of Protection), it's only a matter of time before the person's spouse trusts him or her.

How could Jon be certain that Sue would not have another affair? How could he ever trust her again? It could happen only as they based their relationship on the Rule of Honesty and the Rule of Protection as a demonstration of their trustworthiness. Sue was learning to be completely honest with Jon, and that prevented the creation of a secret second life—an essential ingredient of an affair. She was also firmly committed to taking Jon's feelings into account with every decision she made, and that also made an affair impossible.

Many wayward spouses have demanded that the betrayed spouse trust them. They argue that without that trust their marriage cannot thrive. They are not using that argument to build their marriage, but rather to get their way. They don't follow the Policy of Joint Agreement, asking how their spouse would feel about their decisions but they insist that the spouse trust their judgment. They don't tell their spouse what they are doing in their secret second life but they want the spouse to believe that it is not anything harmful to the marriage. Wanting trust in these situations is simply an effort to get away with thoughtlessness and dishonesty.

But trust can be achieved when a wayward spouse has proven a willingness and ability to follow the Rule of Honesty and the Rule of Protection. A willingness to follow those rules, along with the months that it takes to prove the ability to follow them, creates a trust that does not have to be demanded. It comes effortlessly.

Checklist for Managing Resentment and Restoring Trust

How to Control and Overcome Resentment

_____ Allow time for the memories that trigger resentment to fade (about two years).

_____ Avoid dwelling on the mistakes of the past and focus attention on the present and future. Avoid mistakes in the present that trigger memory of past mistakes and the resentment that comes with those memories.

_____ Avoid using resentment as leverage to get your way in a conflict.

How to Restore Trust

_____ Follow the Rule of Protection.

_____ Follow the Rule of Honesty.

Renewing Marital Commitment

Completing Marital Recovery Part 2

Sue and Jon agreed to follow my four rules to guide their marital recovery when they first began to reconcile. Without these rules, I don't think their marriage would have survived. Couples who try to reconcile without these rules usually fail to address the issues that created the affair in the first place. Before long they find themselves back in the same hopeless marriage, tempted to engage in another affair. But the four rules enabled Sue and Jon to overcome the conditions that made her affair possible. And the new conditions that were created affair-proofed their marriage.

At first, the four rules seemed very restrictive and unnatural. That's true of most things that are new—it takes a while to get used to them. Not only were these rules new for Sue and Jon, they also contradicted most of their instincts. When they first married, they believed that they could trust their instincts. But their instincts had led them to disaster. The four rules did something their instincts couldn't do—led Sue and Jon to marital recovery.

And what a recovery it was! I'll let Sue explain how she felt about it.

Sue's Side of the Story

I'll be honest with you. At first, I didn't believe that any of these little rules would do me any good, but I went along with them because I had no other choice. Greg, the one I thought was my soul mate, had left me because I just couldn't shake my depression, and he finally gave up on me. So with Greg out of the picture, I could either try to get back together with Jon or start a new relationship from the beginning. I couldn't imagine starting a new relationship, so I figured I had nothing to lose by giving Jon a second chance. I figured I owed him at least that. But I had no feelings for him at all. In fact I was repulsed by the idea of being in bed with him again.

The rules we were supposed to follow were easier than I thought, especially since I couldn't be with Greg, even if I was tempted. I realized at the time that if Greg had called to take me back, I would have jumped at the chance to be with him again. But he never called.

Since I was willing to give our marriage a chance, spending time with Jon was what I had expected to do anyway. And the rules made our time together much more enjoyable than it would have been without the rules. These rules were there to keep us from making each other unhappy and they encouraged us to have a good time.

After about a week, I was feeling a lot better about my decision to live with Jon again and I started feeling less depressed. The time we spent together was not exciting but it wasn't unpleasant either. We were not allowed to discuss my affair, and that made everything much less stressful. I couldn't imagine ever loving Jon again but I began to see how we could live together, at least until the children were grown.

The goal for us was passion, something that I just didn't think would ever be possible. For the first few weeks, even though Jon was doing everything by the book, my feelings for him did not change. I thought of him as a friend, but not as a lover. Feeling that he was my friend was encouraging, though.

We continued to follow the rules and spent most of Jon's free time together. At times I resented giving Jon so much of my time but I figured it was a small price to pay if it would really bring our family back together.

Then one day I really felt something for Jon. It was something I hadn't felt for him in years and I was very excited. We made love with passion for the first time in over two years, and I felt as if we had never been away from each other. I loved Jon as much as I had ever loved Greg.

Unfortunately the next day the feeling was gone. Before we had the rules to follow, I would have lied to Jon about my loss of love for him. I used to think it was my marital obligation to tell him I loved him, but I didn't lie this time. I told him that my feelings for him were gone.

Jon handled the situation better than he would have before he knew about the rules. He realized that my feelings for him would eventually return if he kept depositing love units. That put much less pressure on me, and I felt more at ease when we were together.

Then, a few days later, I felt love for Jon again. I was prepared for these cyclic feelings. I was told that when Jon deposited a certain number of love units into his account with me, that would trigger my feeling of love for Jon. When the account was above that point, I would be in love with him, and when it was below that point, the feeling of love would not be there.

And that's exactly what happened. As Jon kept depositing love units, slowly but surely the days I loved Jon increased in number, and the days I didn't love him decreased. I still have a hard time believing that love units could make such a difference in how I feel. I have always cared about Jon but I now understand that my feeling of passion toward him depends on how well he meets my emotional needs. And I also understand why I felt so much passion for Greg. It was because he had met my needs, not because he was really my soul mate. My real soul mate is the man I married, Jon. And now he stirs the same passion in me that Greg used to arouse.

When I felt passion for Greg, I was convinced that he was the one I was meant to be with. Since I did not have the same feeling for Jon, I believed I had married the wrong man. But now I know that Jon was right for me all along.

I don't like to think about the nightmare I've been through. Even now, as I reflect on what happened, I start feeling depressed again. I am so grateful to Jon for waiting for me until I came to my senses. He could have left me because of everything I did. But instead, he kept reaching out to me, and that kept me from falling headlong into a pit that I don't think I could have ever survived. It was his strength that made up for my weakness, and I will always be grateful to him for his patience and commitment to me.

Sue, obviously, was happy with the outcome of their recovery. But what about Jon? How did he feel about everything he'd been through?

Jon's Side of the Story

At first, I was not sure I wanted Sue as my wife. The vision I had of her in bed with Greg made me sick to my stomach. But after I had a chance to think it over, I made a decision to do everything in my power to save our marriage.

At the time, I had no idea what that decision would cost me. And yet, in spite of all of the pain I've felt over the past two years, I would do it all over again for Sue. We both made mistakes and we had to pay for them. We ran the gauntlet and have come through it in love. We are much better people for it. I think our children will greatly benefit from the hard lessons we've learned.

When Sue finally invited me to come back to her, after Greg had left her for another woman, I was very bitter. She chose me because I was the only one left. Then, when I came back, she wouldn't even apologize. She blamed me for her affair. At the time I was ready to feed our new rules to the dog. I felt she owed me a lot and I expected her to welcome me with open arms. My friends thought I was crazy to take Sue back, and there were times that I thought they might be right.

But I had come this far, and I decided to give the rules a chance. My job was to keep my part of the bargain. Avoiding anger, disrespect, and demands was the hardest part. I bit my tongue so often I felt there would be none left.

Being with Sue was all it really took for me to redeposit all the love units that I had withdrawn from her Love Bank. Sue agreed to be with me at least fifteen hours every week, and that time together taught us how to become good friends again. She had always liked my company and our conversation, but I had taken that from her with my career choices. Once her love for me was restored, I knew I could never take it for granted again.

I have finally learned how precious love is. The love Sue and I have for each other is what makes our marriage wonderful. If we didn't have it, I don't think we could survive marriage, in spite of how important it is for our children that we stay together. Now that we have learned how to be in love with each other, I don't think either of us will make the same mistakes again.

In spite of what Sue put me through, I trust her now. That's because I know she loves me and she has put me first in her life. But I also know that following the four rules is what really keeps our marriage safe. It's keeping those rules that makes our trust in each other possible.

The Four Rules of Marriage

The four rules that guided Sue and Jon to recovery also kept their marriage secure long after I saw them for the last time. Once more, I would like to review these rules that make a marriage so successful. The more difficult they are for you to follow, the more important they are for you to learn. That's because without them, you cannot have a fulfilling marriage. And without them, you will certainly fail in your effort to recover after an affair.

> ### The Rule of Protection
> *Avoid being the cause of your spouse's unhappiness.*

You and your spouse were both born with the ability to be angry, disrespectful, and selfish. These are normal traits that I call Love Busters because they destroy the feeling of love couples have for each other. But if you and your spouse follow the Rule of Protection, you avoid being the cause of each other's unhappiness—you do whatever it takes to overcome these destructive tendencies. By eliminating Love Busters, you will not only be protecting your spouse, you will also be preserving your spouse's love for you.

One of the easiest ways to protect your spouse is to follow another rule—the Policy of Joint Agreement: *Never do anything without an enthusiastic agreement between you and your spouse.* By following this Policy you will be reminded that everything you do affects your spouse either positively or negatively, and by getting your spouse's enthusiastic agreement to what you do, you avoid behavior that will cause your spouse to be unhappy. The Policy will also encourage you to negotiate solutions to conflicts that are mutually acceptable, instead of solutions that are good for one and bad for the other. By making mutually acceptable choices, you will create a lifestyle that both of you enjoy.

The Rule of Care
Meet your spouse's most important emotional needs.

You and your spouse fell in love with each other because you met each other's most important emotional needs, and the only way to stay in love is to keep meeting those needs. Even when the feeling of love begins to fade, or when it's gone entirely, it's not necessarily gone for good. It can be recovered whenever you go back to being an expert at depositing love units.

To be an expert at meeting each other's most important needs, you must first know what your spouse's needs are, because they can change from time to time. Then, you must learn to meet those needs in a way that is fulfilling to your spouse, and enjoyable for you too.

The Rule of Time
Take time to give your spouse your undivided attention.

The only way you can meet many of your spouse's important emotional needs is to give your spouse your undivided attention. And if you want it to be a reality instead of a hope, it must be a part of your schedule every week. I suggest that you (a) spend time alone when you give each other your undivided attention; (b) use the time to meet the emotional needs of affection, conversation, recreational companionship, and sexual fulfillment; and (c) plan to schedule at least fifteen hours together each week.

When you were dating, you gave each other this kind of attention and you fell in love. When people have affairs, they also give each other this kind of time and attention to keep their love for each other alive. Why should courtship and affairs be the only times romantic love is created? Why can't it happen in marriage as well? It can, if you set aside time every week to give each other undivided attention.

> ## The Rule of Honesty
> *Be totally open and honest with your spouse.*

Anything short of total honesty isn't honesty. Honesty means being honest with your spouse about your positive and negative emotional reactions, personal history (which includes your weaknesses and strengths), your present schedule, and your thoughts and plans about future activities and objectives. In other words, honesty means never leaving your spouse with false impressions about your thoughts, feelings, habits, likes, dislikes, personal history, daily activities, or plans for the future.

Self-imposed honesty with your spouse is essential to your marriage's safety and success. Honesty will not only bring you closer to each other emotionally, it will also prevent the creation of destructive habits that are kept secret from your spouse. The Rule of Honesty combined with the Policy of Joint Agreement are two guidelines that will help you create an open and integrated lifestyle, one that will guarantee your love for each other.

The Marital Recovery Agreement

To help remind you of the important Rules of Marriage, I have created a Marital Recovery Agreement that you can complete and sign (see appendix D). I encourage you to make an enlarged copy of the Agreement and complete it with your spouse. As indicated in the Agreement, it is to be reviewed several times each year so that you don't forget your commitment to each other.

Jon and Sue completed the Marital Recovery Agreement shortly after I began helping them recover from the affair. They first reviewed the five Love Busters and then identified the ones that needed attention. Sue indicated that Jon needed to avoid disrespectful judgments, and Jon wanted Sue to avoid being dishonest about her feelings and her activities.

To complete the emotional needs section, they had to identify their most important emotional needs and rank the top five in order of their priority.

Finally, Jon and Sue agreed to review their progress regularly to be sure that they were making steady improvement. They also agreed to meet with each other every Sunday afternoon to schedule their fifteen hours of undivided attention for that week.

Jon and Sue took the steps that were necessary to recover from what was the most painful experience of their lives. And those steps brought them to the marriage they had always wanted.

Before I stopped counseling them, Jon admitted that his resentment had faded away, just as I had predicted it would. His trust for Sue grew as her willingness and ability to follow the Policy of Joint Agreement were proven to him. Sue and Jon had fallen in love again and were the soul mates that they had been when they first married.

Kevin and Lee also completed the Marital Recovery Agreement when they began their recovery. And because Kevin had ended his affair before it had spun out of control, it was easier for them to follow the four Rules of Marriage than it had been for Sue and Jon. Lee's resentment faded much more quickly than Jon's did. Within a few months they reported feeling happier with their life and marriage than they had ever been.

A Final Warning: Protect Your Love Bank from the Deposits of Others

If you want a great marriage, you and your spouse must be in love with each other. And if you want to be in love with each other, you must have large balances in each other's Love Bank.

But being in love with each other will not necessarily prevent you from falling in love with someone else. The feeling of love simply means that someone has deposited enough love units in your Love Bank to trigger that feeling. And someone other than your spouse may deposit those love units. But the feeling of love for someone other than your spouse is downright dangerous. Everything in you will encourage you to spend more time with this person who makes you feel so good, even if it is a threat to your spouse. As I have suggested earlier, when you feel attracted to someone of the opposite sex, tell your spouse about it right away, and then avoid being with that person. It's tough to do what Kevin did after he had fallen in love with Amy—he never saw or talked to her again—but it was what he had to do.

> *Make it easy for your spouse, and make it relatively difficult for others, to deposit love units.*

To avoid getting into Kevin's predicament and finding yourself in love with someone else, it's important to guard your Love Bank, keeping others from making too many deposits into it. I suggest extraordinary precautions to protect the Love Bank. Make it easy for your spouse, and make it relatively difficult for others, to deposit love units. You can do that by making sure that no one but your spouse has the opportunity to meet your most important emotional needs. If you want to be in love with your spouse, and avoid being in love with anyone else, see to it that your spouse has the largest account in your Love Bank, and that no one else has a chance to compete.

Here are a few suggestions that will help you guard your Love Bank:

1. Spend most of your recreational time either alone or with your spouse so that when you are having a good time, your spouse is right there enjoying it with you. Avoid recreational activities with members of the opposite sex who could build Love Bank balances by simply being with you when you are enjoying yourself.

2. If you find someone of the opposite sex attractive, avoid spending much time with that person. Avoid dinners together, carpools, business trips, or any other setting that would give the person a chance to deposit enough love units to trigger in you the feeling of romantic love.

3. If someone of the opposite sex ever tells you that he or she finds you attractive, tell that person how much you love your spouse. Never tell that person how you feel about him or her. In general, avoid telling anyone other than your spouse about your attraction to him or her. If that person's feelings of attraction toward you, or your feelings of attraction for him or her, are ever revealed, avoid seeing or talking to that person again.

Many people, following this advice, have spared themselves and their spouse the pain of an affair. These suggestions should not be burdensome to follow. Anyone who has gone through an affair understands that they are only a minor inconvenience when compared to the disaster of infidelity. And these precautions do more than prevent an affair—they also build a stronger emotional bond in the marriage. So they are precautions well worth taking.

> *If you ever find yourself infatuated with someone other than your spouse, don't walk away, RUN!*

If you are attracted to someone of the opposite sex, and you have agreed to the Rule of Protection, you must prevent yourself from forming a romantic relationship with that person. If you ever find yourself infatuated with someone other than your spouse, don't walk away, RUN! Have nothing to do with him or her, even if it means quitting your job, leaving your church, or moving from your neighborhood. And, for sure, don't ever tell him or her how you feel. To do otherwise is to cause your spouse needless pain because it opens up the emotional trap that can lead to an affair.

Looking to the Future

As a marriage counselor, the most rewarding part of counseling a couple is when they start experiencing the rewards of their new habits. I have seen thousands of couples build love and compatibility from the despair that comes from infidelity. These couples recover with a deep emotional attraction and a strong bond for each other. But I warn every couple that this renewed feeling of love depends on their willingness and ability to continue following the four rules that guided them to recovery. It was their ability to protect each other, care for each other, give each other undivided attention, and be completely honest with each other that *caused* these good feelings and their new relationship. To maintain their strong relationship, these four rules must be continually followed.

> *To maintain a strong marital relationship, the four rules must be continually followed.*

Sue and Jon, and Kevin and Lee, like many others, had wondered if they could ever heal from the emotional bruises that the affairs inflicted on them. But in the end, both marriages recovered completely. Both couples created marriages they had always wanted and needed, and the affair, while painful, did not keep them from a lifetime of love.

Checklist for Renewing Marital Commitment

_____ Protect your Love Bank from the deposits of others:

    _____ Spend most of your leisure time with your spouse.

    _____ Avoid spending time with those of the opposite sex whom you find attractive.

    _____ If someone of the opposite sex expresses their attraction to you, respond by expressing the love you have for your spouse and avoid being with that person.

    _____ Never tell someone of the opposite sex, other than your spouse, that you find that person attractive.

_____ Complete the Marital Recovery Agreement in appendix D.

_____ Continue to follow the four rules that guide marital recovery after an affair so that you will maintain a lifelong relationship of love with your spouse.

APPENDIX A

THE MOST IMPORTANT EMOTIONAL NEEDS

Before you complete the Emotional Needs Questionnaire in appendix B, review the following ten most important emotional needs.

Affection

Quite simply, affection is the expression of love. It symbolizes security, protection, comfort, and approval—vitally important ingredients in any relationship. When one spouse is affectionate to the other, the following messages are sent:

1. You are important to me, and I will care for you and protect you.
2. I'm concerned about the problems you face and will be there for you when you need me.

A hug can say those things. When we hug our friends and relatives, we are demonstrating our care for them. And there are other ways to show our affection—a greeting card, an "I love you" note, a bouquet of flowers, holding hands, walks after dinner, back rubs, phone calls, and conversations with thoughtful and loving expressions can all communicate affection.

Affection is, for many, the essential cement of a relationship. Without it many people feel totally alienated. With it they become emotionally bonded. If you feel terrific when your spouse is affectionate and you feel terrible when there is not enough of it, you have the emotional need for affection.

Sexual Fulfillment

We often confuse sex and affection. Affection is an act of love that is nonsexual and can be received from friends, relatives, children, and even pets. However, acts that can show affection, such as hugging and kissing, that are done with a sexual motive are actually sex, not affection.

Most people know whether or not they have a need for sex, but in case there is any uncertainty, I will point out some of the most obvious symptoms.

A sexual need usually predates your current relationship and is somewhat independent of your relationship. While you may have discovered a deep desire to make love to your spouse since you've been in love, it isn't quite the same thing as a sexual need. Wanting to make love when you are in love is sometimes merely a reflection of wanting to be emotionally and physically close.

Sexual fantasies are usually a dead giveaway for a sexual need. Fantasies in general are good indicators of emotional needs—your most common fantasies usually reflecting your most important needs. If you have imagined what it would be like having your sexual need met in the most fulfilling ways, you probably have a sexual need. The more the fantasy is employed, the greater your need. And the way your sexual need is met in your fantasy is usually a good indicator of your sexual predispositions and orientation.

When you married, you and your spouse both promised to be faithful to each other for life. This means that you agreed to be each other's only sexual partner "until death do us part." You made this commitment because you trusted each other to meet your sexual needs, to be sexually available and responsive. The need for sex, then, is a very exclusive need, and if you have it, you will be very dependent on your spouse to meet it for you. You have no other ethical choice.

Conversation

Unlike sex, conversation is not a need that can be met exclusively in marriage. Our need for conversation can be ethically met by almost anyone. But if it is one of your most important emotional needs, whoever meets it best will deposit so many love units, you may fall in love with that person. So if it's your need, be sure that your spouse is the one who meets it the best and most often.

Men and women don't have too much difficulty talking to each other during courtship. That's a time of information gathering for both partners. Both are highly motivated to discover each other's likes and dislikes, personal background, current interests, and plans for the future.

But after marriage many women find that the man who would spend hours talking to her on the telephone, now seems to have lost all interest in talking to her and spends his spare time watching television or reading. If your need for conversation was fulfilled during courtship, you expect it to be met after marriage.

If you see conversation as a practical necessity, primarily as a means to an end, you probably don't have much of a need for it. But if you have a craving just to talk to someone, if you pick up the telephone just because you feel like talking, if you enjoy conversation in its own right, consider conversation to be one of your most important emotional needs.

Recreational Companionship

A need for recreational companionship combines two needs into one: the need to engage in recreational activities and the need to have a companion.

During your courtship, you and your spouse were probably each other's favorite recreational companions. It's not uncommon for women to join men in hunting, fishing, watching football, or other activities they would never choose on their own. They simply want to spend as much time as possible with the men they like and that means going where they go.

The same is true of men. Shopping centers are no strangers to men in love. They will also take their dates out to dinner, watch romantic movies, and attend concerts and plays. They take every opportunity to be with someone they like and try to enjoy the activity to guarantee more dates in the future.

I won't deny that marriage changes a relationship considerably. But does it have to end the activities that helped make the relationship so compatible? Can't a husband's favorite recreational companion be his wife and vice versa?

If recreational activities are important to you and you like to have someone join you for them to be fulfilling, include recreational companionship on your list of needs. Think about it for a moment in terms of the Love Bank. How much do you enjoy these activities and how many love units would your spouse be depositing whenever you enjoyed them together? What a waste it would be if someone else got credit for all those love units! And if it is someone of the opposite sex, it would be downright dangerous.

Who should get credit for all those love units? The one you should love the most, your spouse. That's precisely why I encourage couples to be each other's favorite recreational companions. It's one of the simplest ways to deposit love units.

Honesty and Openness

Most of us want an honest relationship with our spouse. But some of us have a need for such a relationship because honesty and openness give us a sense of security.

To feel secure, we want accurate information about our spouse's thoughts, feelings, habits, likes, dislikes, personal history, daily activities, and plans for the future. If a spouse does not provide honest and open communication, trust can be undermined and the feelings of security can eventually be destroyed. We can't trust the signals that are being sent and we have no foundation on which to build a solid relationship. Instead of adjusting to each other, we feel off balance; instead of growing together, we grow apart.

Aside from the practical considerations of honesty and openness, there are some of us who feel happy and fulfilled when our spouse reveals his or her most private thoughts to us. And we feel very frustrated when they are hidden. That reaction is evidence of an emotional need, one that can and should be met in marriage.

Physical Attractiveness

For many people, physical appearance can become one of the greatest sources of love units. If you have this need, an attractive person will not only get your attention but may distract you from whatever you're doing. In fact that's what may have first drawn you to your spouse—his or her physical appearance.

There are some who consider this need to be temporary and important only in the beginning of a relationship. After a couple get to know each other better, some feel that physical attractiveness should take a backseat to deeper and more intimate needs.

But that's not been my experience, nor has it been the experience of many people whom I've counseled, particularly men. For many, the need for an attractive spouse continues on throughout marriage, and just seeing the spouse looking attractive deposits love units.

Among the various aspects of physical attractiveness, weight generally gets the most attention. However, choice of clothing, hairstyle, makeup, and personal hygiene also come together to make a person attractive. It can be very subjective, and you are the judge of what is attractive to you.

If the attractiveness of your spouse makes you feel great, and loss of that attractiveness would make you feel very frustrated, you should probably include this category on your list of important emotional needs.

Financial Support

People often marry for the financial security that their spouse provides them. In other words, part of the reason they marry is for money. Is financial support one of your important emotional needs?

It may be difficult for you to know how much you need financial support, especially if your spouse has always been gainfully employed. But what if, before marriage, your spouse had told you not to expect any income from him or her? Would it have affected your decision to marry? Or what if your spouse could not find work, and you had to financially support him or her throughout life? Would that withdraw love units?

You may have a need for financial support if you expect your spouse to earn a living. But you definitely have that need if you do not expect to be earning a living yourself, at least during part of your marriage.

What constitutes financial support? Earning enough to buy everything you could possibly desire or earning just enough to get by? Different couples would answer this differently, and the same couples might answer differently in different stages of life. But, like many of these emotional needs, financial support is sometimes hard to talk about. As a result, many couples have hidden expectations, assumptions, and resentments. Try to understand what you expect from your spouse financially to feel fulfilled. And what would it take for you to feel frustrated? Your analysis will help you determine if you have a need for financial support.

Domestic Support

The need for domestic support is a time bomb. At first it seems irrelevant, a throwback to more primitive times. But for many couples, the need explodes after a few years of marriage, surprising both husband and wife.

Domestic support involves the creation of a peaceful and well-managed home environment. It includes cooking meals, washing dishes, washing and ironing clothes, cleaning house, and child care. If you feel very fulfilled when your spouse does these things and very annoyed when they are not done, you have the need for domestic support.

In earlier generations, it was assumed that all husbands had this need and all wives would naturally meet it. Times have changed, and needs have changed along with them. Now many of the men I counsel would rather have their wives meet their needs for affection or conversation, needs that have traditionally been more characteristic of women. And many women, especially career women, gain a great deal of pleasure having their husbands create a peaceful and well-managed home environment.

Marriage usually begins with a willingness of both spouses to share domestic responsibilities. Newlyweds commonly wash dishes together, make the bed together, and divide many household tasks. The groom welcomes his wife's help in doing what he had to do by himself as a bachelor. At this point in marriage, neither of them would identify domestic support as an important emotional need. But the time bomb is ticking.

When does the need for domestic support explode? When the children arrive! Children create huge needs—both a greater need for income and greater domestic responsibilities. The previous division of labor becomes obsolete. Both spouses must take on new responsibilities—and which ones will they take?

At this point in your marriage, you may find no need for domestic support at all. But that may change later when you have children. In fact as soon as you are expecting your first child, you will find yourselves dramatically changing your priorities.

Family Commitment

In addition to a greater need for income and domestic responsibilities, the arrival of children creates in many people the need for family commitment. Again, if you don't have children yet, you may not sense this need, but when the first child arrives, a change may take place that you didn't anticipate.

Family commitment is not just child care—feeding, clothing, or watching over children to keep them safe. Child care falls under the category of domestic support. Family commitment, on the other hand, is a responsibility for the development of the children, teaching them the values of cooperation and care for each other. It is spending quality time with your children to help them develop into successful adults.

Evidence of this need is a craving for your spouse's involvement in the educational and moral development of your children. When he or she is helping care for them, you feel very fulfilled, and when he or she neglects their development, you feel very frustrated.

We all want our children to be successful, but if you have the need for family commitment, your spouse's participation in family activities will deposit carloads of love units. And your spouse's neglect of your children will noticeably withdraw them.

Admiration

If you have the need for admiration, you may have fallen in love with your spouse partly because of his or her compliments to you. Some people just love to be told that they are appreciated. Your spouse may also have been careful not to criticize you. If you have a need for admiration, criticism may hurt you deeply.

Many of us have a deep desire to be respected, valued, and appreciated by our spouse. We need to be affirmed clearly and often. There's nothing wrong with feeling that way. Even God wants us to appreciate him!

Appreciation is one of the easiest needs to meet. Just a compliment, and presto, you've made your spouse's day. On the other hand, it's also easy to be critical. A trivial word of rebuke can be very upsetting to some people, ruining their day and withdrawing love units at an alarming rate.

Your spouse may have the power to build up or deplete his or her account in your Love Bank with just a few words. If you can be affected that easily, be sure to add admiration to your list of important emotional needs.

Appendix B

Emotional Needs Questionnaire

© 1986 by Willard F. Harley, Jr.

Name_____ Date_____

This questionnaire is designed to help you determine your most important emotional needs and evaluate your spouse's effectiveness in meeting those needs. Answer all the questions as candidly as possible. Do not try to minimize any needs that you feel have been unmet. If your answers require more space, use and attach a separate sheet of paper.

Your spouse should complete an Emotional Needs Questionnaire so that you can discover his or her needs and evaluate your effectiveness in meeting those needs.

When you have completed this questionnaire, go through it a second time to be certain your answers accurately reflect your feelings. Do not erase your original answers, but cross them out lightly so that your spouse can see the corrections and discuss them with you.

The final page of this questionnaire asks you to identify and rank five of the ten needs in order of their importance to you. The most important emotional needs are those that give you the most pleasure when met and frustrate you the most when unmet. Resist the temptation to identify as most important only those needs that your spouse is not presently meeting. Include *all* your emotional needs in your consideration of those that are most important.

1. **Affection.** Showing love through words, cards, gifts, hugs, kisses, and courtesies; creating an environment that clearly and repeatedly expresses love.

   A. **Need for affection:** Indicate how much you need affection by circling the appropriate number.

0	1	2	3	4	5	6
I have no need for affection			I have a moderate need for affection			I have a great need for affection

   If or when your spouse *is not* affectionate with you, how do you feel? (Circle the appropriate letter.)
   a. Very unhappy
   b. Somewhat unhappy
   c. Neither happy nor unhappy
   d. Happy not to be shown affection

   If or when your spouse is affectionate to you, how do you feel? (Circle the appropriate letter.)
   a. Very happy
   b. Somewhat happy
   c. Neither happy nor unhappy
   d. Unhappy to be shown affection

   B. **Evaluation of spouse's affection:** Indicate your satisfaction with your spouse's affection toward you by circling the appropriate number.

-3	-2	-1	0	1	2	3
I am extremely dissatisfied			I am neither satisfied nor dissatisfied			I am extremely satisfied

   My spouse gives me all the affection I need.   Yes   No

   If your answer is no, how often would you like your spouse to be affectionate with you?

   _____ (write number) times each day/week/month (circle one).

   I like the way my spouse gives me affection.   Yes   No

   If your answer is no, explain how your need for affection could be better satisfied in your marriage. _____

   _____

   _____

   _____

   _____

   _____

   _____

   _____

2. **Sexual Fulfillment.** A sexual relationship that brings out a predictably enjoyable sexual response in both of you that is frequent enough for both of you.

A. **Need for sexual fulfillment:** Indicate how much you need sexual fulfillment by circling the appropriate number.

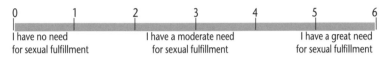

0	1	2	3	4	5	6

I have no need
for sexual fulfillment

I have a moderate need
for sexual fulfillment

I have a great need
for sexual fulfillment

If or when your spouse *is not* willing to engage in sexual relations with you, how do you feel? (Circle the appropriate letter.)
a. Very unhappy
b. Somewhat unhappy
c. Neither happy nor unhappy
d. Happy not to engage in sexual relations

If or when your spouse engages in sexual relations with you, how do you feel? (Circle the appropriate letter.)
a. Very happy
b. Somewhat happy
c. Neither happy nor unhappy
d. Unhappy to engage in sexual relations

B. **Evaluation of sexual relations with your spouse:** Indicate your satisfaction with your spouse's sexual relations with you by circling the appropriate number.

-3	-2	-1	0	1	2	3

I am extremely
dissatisfied

I am neither satisfied
nor dissatisfied

I am extremely
satisfied

My spouse has sexual relations with me as often as I need.   Yes   No

If your answer is no, how often would you like your spouse to have sex with you?

_____ (write number) times each day/week/month (circle one).

I like the way my spouse has sexual relations with me.   Yes   No

If your answer is no, explain how your need for sexual fulfillment could be better satisfied in your marriage. _____
_____
_____
_____
_____
_____

3. **Conversation.** Talking about events of the day, feelings, and plans; avoiding angry or judgmental statements or dwelling on past mistakes; showing interest in your favorite topics of conversation; balancing conversation; using it to inform, investigate, and understand you; and giving you undivided attention.

   A. **Need for conversation:** Indicate how much you need conversation by circling the appropriate number.

|0|1|2|3|4|5|6|

I have no need   I have a moderate need   I have a great need
for conversation   for conversation   for conversation

If or when your spouse *is not* willing to talk with you, how do you feel? (Circle the appropriate letter.)
a. Very unhappy   c. Neither happy nor unhappy
b. Somewhat unhappy   d. Happy not to talk

If or when your spouse talks to you, how do you feel? (Circle the appropriate letter.)
a. Very happy   c. Neither happy nor unhappy
b. Somewhat happy   d. Unhappy to talk

   B. **Evaluation of conversation with your spouse:** Indicate your satisfaction with your spouse's conversation with you by circling the appropriate number.

|-3|-2|-1|0|1|2|3|

I am extremely   I am neither satisfied   I am extremely
dissatisfied   nor dissatisfied   satisfied

My spouse talks to me as often as I need.   Yes   No

If your answer is no, how often would you like your spouse to talk to you?

_____ (write number) times each day/week/month (circle one).

_____ (write number) hours each day/week/month (circle one).

I like the way my spouse talks to me.   Yes   No

If your answer is no, explain how your need for conversation could be better satisfied in your marriage. _____
_____
_____
_____

4. **Recreational Companionship.** Developing interest in your favorite recreational activities, learning to be proficient in them, and joining you in those activities. If any prove to be unpleasant to your spouse after an effort has been made, negotiating new activities that are mutually enjoyable.

A. **Need for recreational companionship:** Indicate how much you need recreational companionship by circling the appropriate number.

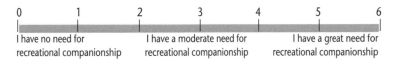

| 0 | 1 | 2 | 3 | 4 | 5 | 6 |

I have no need for recreational companionship   I have a moderate need for recreational companionship   I have a great need for recreational companionship

If or when your spouse *is not* willing to join you in recreational activities, how do you feel? (Circle the appropriate letter.)
a. Very unhappy
b. Somewhat unhappy
c. Neither happy nor unhappy
d. Happy not to include my spouse

If or when your spouse joins you in recreational activities, how do you feel? (Circle the appropriate letter.)
a. Very happy
b. Somewhat happy
c. Neither happy nor unhappy
d. Unhappy to join in recreational activities

B. **Evaluation of recreational companionship with your spouse:** Indicate your satisfaction with your spouse's recreational companionship by circling the appropriate number.

| -3 | -2 | -1 | 0 | 1 | 2 | 3 |

I am extremely dissatisfied   I am neither satisfied nor dissatisfied   I am extremely satisfied

My spouse joins me in recreational activities as often as I need.   Y   N

If your answer is no, how often would you like your spouse to join you in recreational activities?

_____ (write number) times each day/week/month (circle one).

_____ (write number) hours each day/week/month (circle one).

I like the way my spouse joins me in recreational activities.   Yes   No

If your answer is no, explain how your need for recreational companionship could be better satisfied in your marriage. _____
_____
_____

5. **Honesty and Openness.** Revealing positive and negative feelings, events of the past, daily events and schedule, plans for the future; not leaving you with a false impression; answering your questions truthfully.

A. **Need for honesty and openness:** Indicate how much you need honesty and openness by circling the appropriate number.

| 0 | 1 | 2 | 3 | 4 | 5 | 6 |

I have no need
for honesty and openness

I have a moderate need
for honesty and openness

I have a great need
for honesty and openness

If or when your spouse *is not* open and honest with you, how do you feel? (Circle the appropriate letter.)
a. Very unhappy
b. Somewhat unhappy
c. Neither happy nor unhappy
d. Happy not to be honest and open

If or when your spouse is open and honest with you, how do you feel? (Circle the appropriate letter.)
a. Very happy
b. Somewhat happy
c. Neither happy nor unhappy
d. Unhappy to be honest and open

B. **Evaluation of spouse's honesty and openness:** Indicate your satisfaction with your spouse's honesty and openness by circling the appropriate number.

| -3 | -2 | -1 | 0 | 1 | 2 | 3 |

I am extremely
dissatisfied

I am neither satisfied
nor dissatisfied

I am extremely
satisfied

In which of the following areas of honesty and openness would you like to see improvement from your spouse? (Circle the letters that apply to you.)
a. Sharing positive and negative emotional reactions to significant aspects of life
b. Sharing information regarding his/her personal history
c. Sharing information about his/her daily activities
d. Sharing information about his/her future schedule and plans

If you circled any of the above, explain how your need for honesty and openness could be better satisfied in your marriage. _____

_____

_____

_____

_____

_____

_____

6. **Physical attractiveness.** Keeping physically fit with diet and exercise; wearing hair, clothing, and (if female) makeup in a way that you find attractive and tasteful.

A. **Need for an attractive spouse:** Indicate how much you need an attractive spouse by circling the appropriate number.

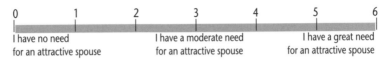

0	1	2	3	4	5	6
I have no need for an attractive spouse			I have a moderate need for an attractive spouse			I have a great need for an attractive spouse

If or when your spouse *is not* willing to make the most of his or her physical attractiveness, how do you feel? (Circle the appropriate letter.)
a. Very unhappy   c. Neither happy nor unhappy
b. Somewhat unhappy   d. Happy he or she does not make an effort

When your spouse makes the most of his or her physical attractiveness, how do you feel? (Circle the appropriate letter.)
a. Very happy   c. Neither happy nor unhappy
b. Somewhat happy   d. Unhappy to see him or her make an effort

B. **Evaluation of spouse's attractiveness:** Indicate your satisfaction with your spouse's attractiveness by circling the appropriate number.

-3	-2	-1	0	1	2	3
I am extremely dissatisfied			I am neither satisfied nor dissatisfied			I am extremely satisfied

In which of the following characteristics of attractiveness would you like to see improvement from your spouse? (Circle the letters that apply.)
a. Physical fitness and normal weight   d. Good physical hygiene
b. Attractive choice of clothes   e. Attractive facial makeup
c. Attractive hairstyle   f. Other _____

If you circled any of the above, explain how your need for an attractive spouse could be better satisfied in your marriage. _____

_____

_____

_____

_____

_____

7. **Financial Support.** Provision of the financial resources to house, feed, and clothe your family at a standard of living acceptable to you, but avoiding travel and working hours that are unacceptable to you.

   A. **Need for financial support:** Indicate how much you need financial support by circling the appropriate number.

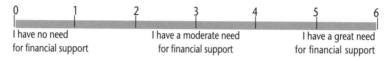

0	1	2	3	4	5	6
I have no need for financial support			I have a moderate need for financial support			I have a great need for financial support

   If or when your spouse *is not* willing to support you financially, how do you feel? (Circle the appropriate letter.)
   a. Very unhappy
   b. Somewhat unhappy
   c. Neither happy nor unhappy
   d. Happy not to be financially supported

   If or when your spouse supports you financially, how do you feel? (Circle the appropriate letter.)
   a. Very happy
   b. Somewhat happy
   c. Neither happy nor unhappy
   d. Unhappy to be financially supported

   B. **Evaluation of spouse's financial support:** Indicate your satisfaction with your spouse's financial support by circling the appropriate number.

-3	-2	-1	0	1	2	3
I am extremely dissatisfied			I am neither satisfied nor dissatisfied			I am extremely satisfied

   How much money would you like your spouse to earn to support you?
   _____

   How many hours each week would you like your spouse to work? _____

   If your spouse is not earning as much as you would like, is not working the hours you would like, does not budget the way you would like, or does not earn an income the way you would like, explain how your need for financial support could be better satisfied in your marriage. _____
   _____
   _____
   _____
   _____
   _____
   _____

8. **Domestic support.** Creation of a home environment for you that offers a refuge from the stresses of life; managing the home and care of the children—if any are at home—including but not limited to cooking meals, washing dishes, washing and ironing clothes, housecleaning.

  A. **Need for domestic support:** Indicate how much you need domestic support by circling the appropriate number.

  If your spouse *is not* willing to provide you with domestic support, how do you feel? (Circle the appropriate letter.)
  a. Very unhappy
  b. Somewhat unhappy
  c. Neither happy nor unhappy
  d. Happy not to have domestic support

  If or when your spouse provides you with domestic support, how do you feel? (Circle the appropriate letter.)
  a. Very happy
  b. Somewhat happy
  c. Neither happy nor unhappy
  d. Unhappy to have domestic support

  B. **Evaluation of spouse's domestic support:** Indicate your satisfaction with your spouse's domestic support by circling the appropriate number.

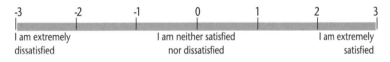

  My spouse provides me with all the domestic support I need.   Yes   No

  I like the way my spouse provides domestic support.   Yes   No

  If your answer is no to either of the above questions, explain how your need for domestic support could be better satisfied in your marriage. _____

  _____
  _____
  _____
  _____
  _____
  _____

9. **Family commitment.** Scheduling sufficient time and energy for the moral and educational development of your children; reading to them, taking them on frequent outings, educating himself or herself in appropriate child-training methods and discussing those methods with you; avoiding any child-training method or disciplinary action that does not have your enthusiastic support.

A. **Need for family commitment:** Indicate how much you need family commitment by circling the appropriate number.

| 0 | 1 | 2 | 3 | 4 | 5 | 6 |

I have no need for family commitment

I have a moderate need for family commitment

I have a great need for family commitment

If or when your spouse *is not* willing to provide family commitment, how do you feel? (Circle the appropriate letter.)
a. Very unhappy
b. Somewhat unhappy
c. Neither happy nor unhappy
d. Happy he/she's not involved

If or when your spouse provides family commitment, how do you feel? (Circle the appropriate letter.)
a. Very happy
b. Somewhat happy
c. Neither happy nor unhappy
d. Unhappy he/she's involved in the family

B. **Evaluation of spouse's family commitment:** Indicate your satisfaction with your spouse's family commitment by circling the appropriate number.

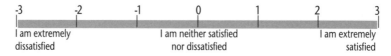

| -3 | -2 | -1 | 0 | 1 | 2 | 3 |

I am extremely dissatisfied

I am neither satisfied nor dissatisfied

I am extremely satisfied

My spouse commits enough time to the family.   Yes   No

If your answer is no, how often would you like your spouse to join in family activities?

_____ (write number) times each day/week/month (circle one).

_____ (write number) hours each day/week/month (circle one).

I like the way my spouse spends time with the family.   Yes   No

If your answer is no, explain how your need for family commitment could be better satisfied in your marriage. _____

_____

10. **Admiration.** Respecting, valuing, and appreciating you; rarely critical and expressing admiration to you clearly and often.

   A. **Need for admiration:** Indicate how much you need admiration by circling the appropriate number.

```
0          1          2          3          4          5          6
I have no need             I have a moderate need            I have a great need
for admiration                for admiration                    for admiration
```

   If or when your spouse *does not* admire you, how do you feel? (Circle the appropriate letter.)
   a. Very unhappy   c. Neither happy nor unhappy
   b. Somewhat unhappy   d. Happy not to be admired

   If or when your spouse does admire you, how do you feel? (Circle the appropriate letter.)
   a. Very happy   c. Neither happy nor unhappy
   b. Somewhat happy   d. Unhappy to be admired

   B. **Evaluation of spouse's admiration:** Indicate your satisfaction with your spouse's admiration of you by circling the appropriate number.

```
-3        -2        -1         0         1         2         3
I am extremely            I am neither satisfied            I am extremely
dissatisfied                nor dissatisfied                   satisfied
```

   My spouse gives me all the admiration I need.   Yes   No

   If your answer is no, how often would you like your spouse to admire you? _____ times each day/week/month (circle one).

   I like the way my spouse admires me.   Yes   No

   If your answer is no, explain how your need for admiration could be better satisfied in your marriage. _____

   _____

   _____

   _____

   _____

   _____

   _____

   _____

   _____

   _____

   _____

   _____

Ranking of Your Emotional Needs

The ten basic emotional needs are listed below. There is also space for you to add other emotional needs that you feel are essential to your marital happiness.

In the space provided in front of each need, write a number from 1 to 5 that ranks the need's importance to your happiness. Write a 1 before the most important need, a 2 before the next most important, and so on until you have ranked your five most important needs.

To help you rank these needs, imagine that you will have only one need met in your marriage. Which would make you the happiest, knowing that all the others would go unmet? That need should be 1. If only two needs will be met, what would your second selection be? Which five needs, when met, would make you the happiest?

_____ Affection

_____ Sexual fulfillment

_____ Conversation

_____ Recreational companionship

_____ Honesty and openness

_____ Physical attractiveness

_____ Financial support

_____ Domestic support

_____ Family commitment

_____ Admiration

_____ _____

_____ _____

_____ _____

_____ _____

Personal History Questionnaire

© 1998 by Willard F. Harley, Jr.

Name_____ Date_____

Please answer all of the following questions as honestly and thoughtfully as possible. If your answer requires additional space, use another sheet of paper.

When answering these questions, it is important to remember the Rule of Honesty and its five parts:

The Rule of Honesty for Successful Marriage

Reveal to your spouse as much information about yourself as you know—your thoughts, feelings, habits, likes, dislikes, personal history, daily activities, and plans for the future

1. *Emotional honesty:* Reveal your emotional reactions—both positive and negative—to the events of your life, particularly to your spouse's behavior.

2. *Historical honesty:* Reveal information about your personal history, particularly events that demonstrate personal weakness and failure.
3. *Current honesty:* Reveal information about the events of your day. Provide your spouse with a calendar of your activities, with special emphasis on those that may affect your spouse.
4. *Future honesty:* Reveal your thoughts and plans regarding future activities and objectives.
5. *Complete honesty:* Do not leave your spouse with a false impression about your thoughts, feelings, habits, likes, dislikes, personal history, daily activities, or plans for the future. Do not deliberately keep personal information from your spouse.

I agree to consider this information confidential and will not share any information revealed in this questionnaire to anyone without my spouse's permission. I also agree to reward honesty and not punish my spouse for revealing any new information to me that I may find upsetting.

Signature: _____

Health History

List childhood diseases, injuries, or operations:

_____

_____

List past adult diseases, injuries, or operations:

_____

_____

List present medical problems (include high blood pressure, arthritis, migraine headaches, etc.):

_____

_____

_____

When did you have your last complete physical examination?

_____

What were the results? Did the doctor find a medical problem or are you generally in good health?

_____

_____

How long does it usually take you to fall asleep when you go to bed at night? ____ How many hours do you usually sleep?____

How often do you awaken during the night?_____
How long does it take to get back to sleep? _____

How many pounds have you gained and/or lost in the past year?

_____

_____

Describe any of your past and present diet programs:

_____

_____

_____

Describe your current exercise program:

_____

_____

_____

What drugs do you presently take, what dosages, how often, and for what conditions?

_____

_____

_____

Have you ever been hospitalized or received therapy for a mental disorder? If so, list hospital(s) and/or therapist(s) and approximate dates:

_____

_____

Do you now have or have you ever had venereal disease? If so, when and what were the conditions?

_____

_____

_____

For the wife: When did you have your first period? _____ Are your periods regular? _____ Are they comfortable? _____ Do they cause you to feel depressed, anxious, or irritable? _____

Family History

Mother's name: _____

age:_____ occupation:_____ education: _____

How did she punish you?

_____

_____

How did she reward you?

_____

_____

What behaviors did she punish?

_____

_____

What behaviors did she reward?

_____

_____

How would others describe your mother?

_____

_____

How would you describe your mother?

_____

_____

What activities did you do with your mother when you were a child?

_____

_____

How did you get along with your mother?

_____

_____

_____

Father's name: _____

age:_____ occupation:_____ education: _____

How did he punish you?

_____

_____

How did he reward you?

_____

_____

What behaviors did he punish?

_____

_____

What behaviors did he reward?

_____

_____

How would others describe your father?

_____

_____

How would you describe your father?

_____

_____

What activities did you do with your father when you were a child?

_____

_____

How did you get along with your father?

_____

_____

For each of your brother(s) and sister(s), give name, birth date, and how you got along with him/her when you were growing up together:

_____

_____

_____

Does (did) your mother or father favor one child? If so, who and why do you think they favored that child?

_____

_____

Were your mother and father divorced? If so, how old were you and what do you know about the reasons they divorced?

_____

_____

How do (did) your mother and father get along?

_____

_____

Was your father or mother (or both) alcoholic? If so, how did it affect your childhood?

_____

_____

Describe any instances of physical violence or sexual advances inflicted on you by a parent or siblings when you were a child.

_____

_____

_____

If you were raised by a stepparent or foster parents, please describe your most important experiences with them.

_____

_____

_____

_____

Educational History

What preschool(s) did you attend?

_____

Describe any significant experiences there:

_____

_____

What elementary school(s) did you attend?

_____

Were you a good student?_____ Describe any significant experiences at your elementary school:

_____

_____

What middle and/or secondary school(s) did you attend?

_____

What were your grades?_____ Describe any significant experiences at your middle school or secondary school:

_____

_____

What college(s) or vocational school(s) did you attend?

_____

What were your grades?_____ Describe any significant experiences at college or vocational school:

_____

_____

What was your major or specialization?_____

Give degree and date earned: _____

What postgraduate school(s) did you attend?

_____

What were your grades?_____ Describe any significant experiences in postgraduate school:

_____

_____

What was your major? _____

Give degree and date earned: _____

Describe sports or other extracurricular activities in which you participated, awards you received, and musical instruments you played, throughout your education.

_____

_____

_____

What are your future educational plans?

_____

_____

Vocational History

List the jobs you have held, giving the present or most recent job first. For each job, give the dates you were employed, your job title and salary, and what you liked and disliked about the job.

_____

_____

_____

_____

_____

How often do you miss work at jobs you enjoy? _____

At jobs you dislike? _____

Describe how well you get along with your fellow employees?

_____

Describe how well you get along with your supervisor(s)?

_____

What training or education have you had that is relevant to your present occupation?

_____

Does your job satisfy you intellectually? Y/N   emotionally? Y/N   physically? Y/N

What are your vocational ambitions?

_____

_____

What were your childhood interests and hobbies?

_____

_____

What are your present leisure time interests and hobbies?

_____

_____

Religious History

What is the name of your religion?

_____

Describe your most important religious beliefs.

_____

_____

How do your religious beliefs influence the decisions you make in your life?

_____

_____

List your religious activities (prayer, study, meetings, etc.) and how frequently you participate in each one:

_____

_____

Describe how your religious beliefs and those of your parents affected your childhood?

_____

_____

Describe any differences between your religious beliefs and those of your spouse:

_____

_____

_____

Describe any important changes in your religious beliefs during your lifetime.

_____

_____

_____

_____

_____

Opposite Sex Relationship History

List all **significant** opposite-sex relationships you had prior to high school and give the person's name, your age and the person's age during the relationship, and the duration of the relationship. Indicate if you were in love and if you had a sexual relationship (use separate sheet of paper if needed):

_____

_____

_____

_____

_____

_____

_____

List all **significant** opposite-sex relationships you had during high school and give the person's name, your age and the person's age during the relationship, and the duration of the relationship. Indicate if you were in love and if you had a sexual relationship (use separate sheet of paper if needed):

_____

_____

_____

_____

_____

_____

_____

List all **significant** opposite-sex relationships you had after high school and give the person's name, your age and the person's age during the relationship, and the duration of the relationship. Indicate if you were in love and if you had a sexual relationship (use separate sheet of paper if needed):

_____

_____

_____

_____

_____

_____

_____

If you have been divorced, give the name of your former spouse, date married, date divorced, reason for divorce, what you liked most and disliked most about the person, and the names and birth dates of children (use seperate sheet of paper if needed):

_____

_____

_____

_____

_____

_____

If you have been widowed, give the name of your spouse, date married, date and cause of spouse's death, what you liked most and disliked most about your spouse, and the names and birth dates of children (use separate sheet of paper if needed):

_____

_____

_____

_____

_____

_____

Sexual History

When and how did you first learn about sex?

_____

_____

_____

How did your parents influence your attitude regarding sex?

_____

_____

_____

What was your parents' attitude concerning sex? (circle one of the following)
1. Sex was shameful and not to be discussed.
2. Sex was not shameful but it wasn't discussed.
3. Sex was shameful but was also discussed.
4. Sex was not shameful and was freely discussed.

Describe your first sexual experience:

_____

_____

_____

_____

Describe your most important sexual experiences and how they influenced the way you think about sex today:

_____

_____

_____

_____

_____

When and how did you first experience sexual arousal and how did you feel about it?

_____

_____

_____

_____

_____

When and how did you first experience sexual climax and how did you feel about it?

_____

_____

_____

If you have ever masturbated, when did you start? _____

How often did you masturbate during childhood?_____

During adolescence? _____

What sexual fantasies do you have when you masturbate?

_____

_____

_____

When did you first have sexual intercourse and how did the experience affect you?

_____

_____

_____

With how many people have you had sexual intercourse? _____

Have you ever:

   had sexual experiences with or fantasies about being treated
      violently? Y/N

   had sexual experiences with or fantasies about treating others
      violently? Y/N

   exposed yourself or desired to expose yourself in public? Y/N

   had sexual contact with children or desired to have sexual contact with
      children? Y/N

Have you ever been in legal trouble because of your sexual behavior? If so, please describe the behavior and circumstances.

_____

_____

_____

_____

_____

Have you ever had an extramarital sexual relationship(s)? If so, please describe it.

_____

_____

_____

Have you ever had a homosexual experience(s)? If so, please describe it.

_____

_____

_____

Personal Assessment

Describe some of your fears:

_____

_____

_____

Describe faults you think you have:

_____

_____

_____

Describe your good characteristics:

_____

_____

_____

If you ever have any of the thoughts given below, check the frequency of occurrence:

Type of thought	hardly ever	occasionally	frequently
I am lonely.	_____	_____	_____
The future is hopeless.	_____	_____	_____
Nobody cares about me.	_____	_____	_____
I feel like killing myself.	_____	_____	_____
I am a failure.	_____	_____	_____

I am intellectually inferior. _____ _____ _____

I am going to faint. _____ _____ _____

I am going to panic. _____ _____ _____

People don't usually like me. _____ _____ _____

Other negative thoughts you may have occasionally or frequently:

_____

_____

Indicate the degree that the following problems are a concern to you using this scale:

> X = concern in the past, not now
>
> 0 = never a concern
>
> 1 = very slight degree of concern
>
> 2 = mild degree of concern
>
> 3 = moderate degree of concern
>
> 4 = severe degree of concern
>
> 5 = very severe degree of concern

sadness _____

suicidal feelings _____

loss of energy _____

low self-esteem _____

isolation and loneliness _____

sleep disturbance _____

headaches _____

dizziness _____

angry feelings _____

mood swings _____

verbal or emotional abuse _____

physical abuse _____

sexual abuse _____

financial problems _____

career problems _____

marital problems _____

parent/child problems _____

Goals for Personal Improvement

Below is a list of bad habits and uncomfortable feelings that may include some that are making you feel anxious and depressed. Check off any habits or uncomfortable feelings that you would like to change:

_____ drinking alcoholic beverages too much

_____ smoking too much

_____ using drugs too much—name the drug(s) _____

_____ eating too much

_____ exercising too little

_____ feeling too much attraction to members of my own sex

_____ feeling too much attraction to members of the opposite sex

_____ feeling nauseated when nervous

_____ thinking depressing thoughts

_____ feeling anxious in crowds

_____ feeling anxious in high places

_____ worrying about my health

_____ feeling anxious in airplanes

_____ stuttering

_____ washing my hands too often

_____ cleaning and straightening things up too often

_____ biting my fingernails

_____ being careless of my physical appearance

_____ feeling anxious in enclosed places

_____ feeling anxious in open places

_____ being too afraid of blood

_____ feeling anxious about contamination or germs

_____ feeling anxious about being alone

_____ feeling afraid of darkness

_____ feeling afraid of certain animals

_____ thinking the same thoughts over and over

_____ counting my heartbeats

_____ hearing voices

_____ feeling people are against me or out to get me

_____ seeing visions or objects that aren't really there

_____ wetting the bed at night or having difficulty controlling my bladder

_____ having difficulty controlling my bowel movement

_____ taking too much medicine

_____ having too many headaches

_____ gambling too much

_____ being unable to fall asleep at night

_____ exposing my body to strangers

_____ wearing clothes of the opposite sex

_____ feeling sexually attracted to other people's clothing or belongings

_____ feeling sexually attracted to children

_____ feeling sexually attracted to animals

_____ feeling a sexual desire to hurt other people

_____ feeling a sexual desire to be hurt or humiliated

_____ feeling a nonsexual desire to hurt other people

_____ feeling a nonsexual desire to be hurt or humiliated

_____ stealing or a desire to steal

_____ lying

_____ yelling at people when I'm angry

_____ poor management of money

_____ saying foolish things to people

_____ having difficulty carrying on a conversation with people

_____ bothering or irritating people too much

_____ forgetfulness

_____ contemplating suicide

_____ setting fires or a desire to set fires

_____ difficulty being steadily employed

_____ feeling uncomfortable at work

_____ swearing

_____ being too upset when criticized by others

_____ having difficulty expressing feelings

_____ putting things off that need to be done

_____ thinking things that cause guilty feelings

_____ feeling anxious when work is being supervised

____ feeling anxious about sexual thoughts

____ feeling anxious about kissing

____ feeling anxious about petting

____ feeling anxious about sexual intercourse

____ having difficulty making decisions when they need to be made

____ feeling uncomfortable with groups of people

____ feeling anxious about: _____

_____

_____

____ feeling depressed about: _____

_____

_____

____ feeling guilty about: _____

_____

_____

____ being unable to control my desire to: _____

_____

_____

How do you plan to change the habits and/or uncomfortable feelings checked above?

_____

_____

_____

_____

_____

MARITAL RECOVERY AGREEMENT

© 1992 by Willard F. Harley, Jr.

This **Agreement** is made the _____ day of _____, _____, between _____, hereinafter called "husband," and _____, hereinafter called "wife," whereby it is mutually agreed:

I. The husband and wife agree to follow the **Rule of Protection**— Avoid being the cause of your spouse's unhappiness.

   A. To avoid making thoughtless decisions, the husband and wife agree to follow the **Policy of Joint Agreement:** *Never do anything without an enthusiastic agreement between you and your spouse.* This policy guarantees that one spouse will not gain at the other's expense.

   B. To avoid thoughtless behavior, the husband and wife agree to protect each other from the following Love Busters:

      1. ANGRY OUTBURSTS: Deliberate attempts to hurt the other because of anger, usually in the form of verbal or physical attacks. If angry outbursts occur, the husband and wife will follow a course of action that identifies angry

outbursts, investigates their motives and causes, keeps a record of their occurrences, and eliminates them.

2. DISRESPECTFUL JUDGMENTS: Attempts to change the other's attitudes, beliefs, and behavior by trying to force his/her way of thinking through lecture, ridicule, threat, or other means. If disrespectful judgments occur, the husband and wife will follow a course of action that identifies disrespectful judgments, investigates their causes, keeps a record of their occurrences, and eliminates the behavior.

3. SELFISH DEMANDS: Attempts to force the other to do something with implied threat of punishment if he or she refuses. If selfish demands occur, the husband and wife will follow a course of action that identifies selfish demands, investigates their causes, keeps a record of their occurrences, and replaces them with thoughtful requests.

II. The husband and wife agree to follow the **Rule of Care**—Meet your spouse's most important emotional needs.

A. The husband and wife will follow the Rule of Care by identifying each other's emotional needs and selecting at least five that are most important to the husband and at least five that are most important to the wife. Those needs may include the following:

1. AFFECTION: Expressing love in words, cards, gifts, hugs, kisses and courtesies; creating an environment that clearly and repeatedly expresses love.

2. SEXUAL FULFILLMENT: Understanding one's own sexual response and that of the spouse; learning to bring out the best of that response in each other so that their sexual relationship is mutually satisfying and enjoyable.

3. CONVERSATION: Setting aside time each day to talk to each other about events of the day, feelings, and plans; avoiding angry or judgmental statements or dwelling on past mistakes; showing interest in the spouse's favorite topics of conversation; balancing conversation, using it to

inform, investigate, and understand each other; and giving each other undivided attention.

4. RECREATIONAL COMPANIONSHIP: Developing an interest in the favorite recreational activities of the spouse; learning to be proficient in them and joining in those activities; if they prove to be unpleasant after an effort has been made, negotiating with the spouse new recreational activities that are mutually enjoyable.

5. FINANCIAL SUPPORT: Assuming responsibility to house, feed, and clothe the family at a standard of living acceptable to the spouse, but avoiding working hours and travel that is unacceptable to the spouse.

6. PHYSICAL ATTRACTIVENESS: Keeping physically fit with diet and exercise; wearing hair and clothing in a way that the spouse finds attractive and tasteful.

7. HONESTY AND OPENNESS: Describing one's own positive and negative feelings, events of one's past, daily events and schedule, and plans for the future; never leaving the other with a false impression; answering the spouse's questions truthfully and completely.

8. DOMESTIC SUPPORT: Creating a home environment that offers a refuge from the stresses of life; managing the home and care of the children in a way that encourages the spouse to be in the home enjoying the family.

9. FAMILY COMMITMENT: Scheduling sufficient time and energy for the moral and educational development of the children; reading to them, taking them on frequent outings, educating oneself in appropriate child-training methods and discussing those methods with the spouse; avoiding any child-training method of disciplinary action that does not have the enthusiastic support of the spouse.

10. ADMIRATION: Understanding and appreciating one's spouse more than anyone else; never criticizing but showing profound respect and pride.

The husband's five most important emotional needs ranked in order are:

1. _____

2. _____

3. _____

4. _____

5. _____

The wife's five most important emotional needs ranked in order are:

1. _____

2. _____

3. _____

4. _____

5. _____

B. The husband and wife will follow the Rule of Care by creating plans to help form new habits that will meet their spouse's five needs.

C. The husband and wife will follow the Rule of Care by evaluating the success of their plans, creating new plans if the first are unsuccessful; learning to meet new marital needs if their spouse replaces any of the original five with new needs. They will meet every _____ (month, quarter, year) to review this agreement and change it if needed.

III. The husband and wife agree to the **Rule of Time**—Take time to give your spouse your undivided attention. They will do this by:

A. Insuring privacy, planning time together that does not include children, relatives, or friends so that undivided attention is maximized.

B. Using the time together to meet the needs of affection, sexual fulfillment, conversation, and recreational companionship.

C. Committing to spend the number of hours that reflects the quality of the marriage: Fifteen hours each week if the marriage is mutually satisfying, and more time if marital dissatisfaction is reported by either spouse.

D. Scheduling time to be together prior to each week and keeping a record of the time actually spent.

IV. The husband and wife agree to the **Rule of Honesty**—Be totally open and honest with your spouse. They will do this by being:

A. EMOTIONALLY HONEST: Revealing to each other their emotional reactions—both positive and negative—to the events of their lives, particularly to each other's behavior.

B. HISTORICALLY HONEST: Revealing information about their personal histories, particularly events that demonstrate personal weaknesses or failures.

C. CURRENTLY HONEST: Revealing information about the events of their day, providing each other with a calendar of their activities, with special emphasis on those that may affect each other.

D. HONEST ABOUT THE FUTURE: Revealing their thoughts and plans about future activities and objectives.

E. **Completely honest:** Not leaving each other with a false impression about their thoughts, feelings, habits, likes, dislikes, personal history, daily activities, or plans for the future; not keeping any personal information from each other.

In witness whereof, the parties hereto have signed this agreement on the day and year first above written:

_____   _____
Husband   Wife

ABOUT THE AUTHORS

Willard F. Harley, Jr., Ph.D., and his daughter, Jennifer Harley Chalmers, Ph.D., are licensed psychologists and marriage counselors. For the past eight years they have collaborated to create and improve methods that restore love to marriages. Their primary effort has focused on the recovery of marriage following an affair. In *Surviving an Affair* they describe the methods they have found to be most effective in achieving this goal.

Dr. Harley is the author of the best-selling *His Needs, Her Needs: Building an Affair-proof Marriage*. His popular web site address is: http://www.marriagebuilders.com. He and Joyce, his wife of thirty-six years, live in White Bear Lake, Minnesota.

Dr. Chalmers and Phil, her husband of fourteen years, have two daughters and live in Vadnais Heights, Minnesota.

His Needs, Her Needs: Building an Affair-proof Marriage

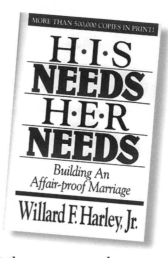

In a successful marriage, a husband and wife meet each other's emotional needs. But when these needs are not met in marriage, a husband and wife are tempted to go outside the marriage to satisfy them.

Ignorance of what these emotional needs are often contributes to a couple's failure to meet them. Men try to meet needs that they value, and women do the same. The needs of men and women, however, are often very different, and husbands and wives end up trying to meet the wrong needs.

In *His Needs, Her Needs* Dr. Harley describes ten important emotional needs for men and women. He helps you identify which are the most important to you and your spouse, explains how to communicate your needs to each other, and guides you in learning how to meet each other's needs.

A successful marriage requires skill in caring for the one you promised to cherish throughout life. *His Needs, Her Needs* will teach you how to care for your spouse, eliminating the major cause of infidelity. Once you have learned the lessons in *His Needs, Her Needs,* your spouse will find you irresistible.

(Hardcover—216 pages)
0-8007-1478-4 Retail $16.99

His Needs, Her Needs is available in condensed form on two 90-minute audiotapes.

0-8007-4400-4 Retail $14.99

Love Busters: Overcoming Habits That Destroy Romantic Love

Love Busters are habits that destroy romantic love. They usually develop soon after marriage and, before long, destroy intimacy, safety, trust . . . and romantic love.

In *Love Busters* Dr. Harley shows couples how to avoid losing romantic love by recognizing and overcoming five common but dangerous Love Busters: angry outbursts, disrespectful judgments, annoying behavior, selfish demands, and dishonesty. When these are unchecked, consideration and thoughtfulness turn into self-centeredness and thoughtlessness. Romantic love is the victim and with it goes all hope for a fulfilling marriage.

Romantic love is not the only victim, however. Dr. Harley also demonstrates how Love Busters prevent couples from resolving common marital conflicts involving friends and relatives, career choices, financial planning, children, and sex. When Love Busters are overcome, these conflicts are easily resolved.

(Hardcover—192 pages)
0-8007-1739-2 Retail $16.99

Five Steps to Romantic Love: A Workbook *for Readers of* Love Busters *and* His Needs, Her Needs

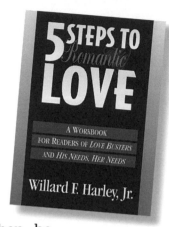

Marriage can last a lifetime if couples apply two rules to their relationships: (1) Meet each other's most important emotional needs, and (2) avoid hurting each other. Dr. Harley wrote the international best-seller *His Needs, Her Needs* to help couples learn to identify and meet each other's most important emotional needs. Then, he wrote *Love Busters* to help couples learn to avoid being the cause of each other's unhappiness.

Now he has written *Five Steps to Romantic Love* to help couples apply the principles found in his first two books. The contracts, questionnaires, inventories, and worksheets that Dr. Harley has used in his counseling practice are arranged in a logical sequence to help couples follow five steps:

1. Make a commitment to overcome marital conflicts.
2. Identify habits that cause unhappiness.
3. Learn to overcome those habits.
4. Identify the most important emotional needs.
5. Learn to meet those needs.

Follow these *Five Steps to Romantic Love* and you'll be on the road to a marriage that is passionate and free of conflict. It's well worth the effort.

(Paperback—192 pages)
0-8007-5623-1 Retail $12.99

Give and Take: The Secret to Marital Compatibility

Most couples begin marriage blissfully compatible and deeply in love. But they usually don't stay that way. Why?

In *Give and Take* you will find out why you and your spouse may have lost the compatibility you had when you married. Then you will learn how to restore it, making you as much in love with each other as you ever were.

You will learn about your Giver and Taker (and about your spouse's Giver and Taker). They certainly can wreak havoc on your marriage, but you can educate these characters and turn them into heroes.

You will become acquainted with the Three States of Marriage and realize how tough it is to negotiate in any of them. Although they can prevent you from getting what you need, their destructive influence can be overcome, and you'll learn how to do it.

By learning how to give and take fairly and effectively, you can give your spouse what he or she needs the most and in return take what you need the most. The lessons of *Give and Take* will make your marriage what it was meant to be—a safe and caring relationship that brings out the best in both of you.

(Hardcover—304 pages)
0-8007-1726-0 Retail $16.99

Give and Take is also available in condensed form on two 90-minute audiotapes. Questionnaires are not included, but all of the essential concepts in their original form are preserved.

0-8007-4405-5 Retail $14.99

Your Love and Marriage: Dr. Harley Answers Your Most Personal Questions

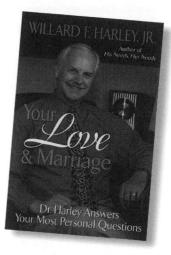

Dr. Harley's popular web site, Marriage Builders, has helped thousands of couples learn to resolve marital conflicts. First they become familiar with basic concepts, and then they read the weekly Q&A columns that deal most closely with the conflict they are experiencing. In each of these Q&A columns, Dr. Harley posts questions he has received regarding a particular marital problem and provides his solution to the problem. If the existing Q&A columns do not help a couple solve their problem, they ask Dr. Harley by e-mail for his personal help in finding a strategy that will work for them. These letters and his answers are sometimes included in new Q&A columns.

Your Love and Marriage is a collection of the most important information found on the Marriage Builders web site. It contains a summary of Dr. Harley's basic concepts, which are followed by the questions he is most frequently asked, and his answers to them. The questions are arranged by topic: How to survive infidelity, sexual adjustment, how to negotiate in marriage, living together before marriage, and how to keep love in your marriage. Under each topic, specific questions are discussed, such as:

- What should I do with my unfaithful spouse?
- Can one spouse save a marriage?
- Why don't I want to make love to my spouse anymore?
- How can I stop the affair I'm having?
- Would living together prepare me for marriage?
- How should we divide domestic responsibilities?

These and scores of other questions are answered in a concise and practical way, showing how Dr. Harley's basic concepts can solve any marital conflict.

Read *Your Love and Marriage* to find the answers to your questions about marriage. Let Dr. Harley's approach to solving marital problems help you solve yours.

(Paperback—320 pages)
0-8007-5642-8 Retail $12.99